Still Beautiful

The Still Beautiful Documentary
and Stories from Kelly's friends

Compiled by Kelly Falardeau
International Speaker, Best-Selling Author
& Burn Survivor

"Still Beautiful is something everyone needs to read. The words resonate with me, I someone who was bullied as a child and adult. I had the same self-confidence issues because being called ugly just becomes believable. Kelly has a way of inspiring people to see her real beauty. In today's society there are too many young people who can learn that beauty doesn't come from the outside shell. It comes from how you and others see you in the inside."

By Lisa Adams

"Kelly is a magnet for the assembly of once-broken beautiful souls. Powered by her own history of pain, struggle, and overcoming, Kelly invites others to share their unique tales of strife and victory. "Still Beautiful" might prove the catalyst for you to start your own self-esteem renovations, or better, perhaps act as the impetus for the telling of your own tale, the writing of your own book."

By Sheree Zielke

"Still Beautiful and Kelly Falardeau's ability to provide confidence for those who are seeking healing from various traumas from physical, emotional and spiritual challenges. Life circumstances and unforeseen addictions that have left each individual with obstacles to champion and create new pathways of healing and self-talk new tools are found in this book. We were all born beautiful and remain beautiful because we are all God's creation even with our battleground of bruises, scars and unseen thoughts we will persevere in living with peace, harmony, truth and falling in love with one's self." By Jacqui Russell

I remember meeting Kelly in grade two. She was really sweet and always wore such pretty dresses. I remember having to line up and all hold hands cause we were going somewhere for class and only then realizing Kelly was different and from then on, trying to make sure I didn't end up beside Kelly so I wouldn't have to hold her hand, looking back I was definitely one of the kids who had fear of 'differences' and Kelly really was the first person I'd encountered who was burnt (breaks my heart writing this). My Dad was friends with Kelly's dad and it was only until my dad told me what had happened did I realize Kelly was just a little girl like me who had a really bad accident with fire. Last time I saw Kelly it was at McDonald's and we sat and had our lunches together. Thoroughly enjoyed "Still Beautiful" and highly recommend the read. By Sharon Hall

"I just finished Kelly's book and I am once again reminded of how proud I am of my friend! When I first met her in grade seven, of course I noticed the scars, but they quickly disappeared in my eyes because she has always been an amazing person, even at such a tender age. Somehow I always knew she would make a difference in people's lives. She gives of herself, whole heartedly, by being open and honest, despite being continuously hurt by a judgemental society. Anyone who takes the time to talk to her and get to know her will realize

that she is an angel on earth! This book is an important read for anyone who struggles with self esteem (who doesn't?) as it is full of inspiration from Kelly and a large handful of contributors who each have helpful and very worthy insight into the true meaning of beauty. My personal paradigm has shifted for the better after reading this book. Bravo Kelly! Keep fighting for a gentler and kinder society!"   By Diane Warrner-Dion

"Still Beautiful is an endearing read of facing adversity with grace and integrity. Kelly has so thoughtfully accounted her journey as she faces life after enduring a tragic incident as a very young child. Its definitely a must read to gain a refreshing view on beauty in our society"   By Bridget Arndt

"Loved Still Beautiful! A great heartfelt open honest story. It's spoke to my heart and I love the way others included their stories as well."   By Shannon Verheist

"The stories within are an inspiration to readers who may learn from and make change in their own life. I like that many of the authors can be contacted for info and help if their story resonates with a reader. It is an easy read with stories so many people can relate to...both young and older. Thanks for this opportunity to have read the book before it final printing. are truly a blessing Kelly."   By Sharyon Broussard

"This book was very inspiring. We think we have problems till we read of others. Thank you for your contribution to the world of burn/depressed people, Beautifully written."   By Brenda Ralph

"This is a very inspirational book. Once I started it I was not able to put it down. Each story, starting with Kelly's, added a new insight on how we are all beautiful. Each of us just needs to find, inside, what that beauty is and let it shine forth for the world to see. Once those around you see that beauty, and accepts that it is yours and yours alone, there will be nothing holding you back. Thank you Kelly for sharing your story and bringing together all the other wonderful stories into your book."   By Don Syms

"Loved your book. I love the style you write it in! Cool with the different characters and the stories in the later half. This book really makes one see and believe what happiness and true beauty really is. It's healing those inside scars and being true to yourself. The AMAZING Kelly you're still beautiful- always have been!"   By Brenda Davidson

DEDICATION

This book is dedicated to my three beautiful kids on earth -- Alexanna, Cody and Parker -- and my Angel baby in heaven, Aleisha.

"No one has the right to take away your power and make you feel ugly. You will always be beautiful no matter what anyone else says."

~Love you all Mom

SPECIAL THANK YOUS TO:
- Every person who participated in the documentary, you are the ones who made it so special.
- Everyone who skydived and/or sponsored a skydiver at the Jump for Kamp Kids.
- Chris McEnroe and Ellen Chloe Bateman of Chalkboard Media who produced this wonderful "Still Beautiful" documentary – www.ChalkboardMedia.ca
- Dr. Barry Lycka who does laser surgery on my scars for free – www.BarryLyckaMD.com
- Darren (and his tandem masters) from Skydive Big Sky – Innisfail www.SkyDiveBigSky.ca
- Our first broadcaster Accessible Media Incorporated. www.AMI.ca
- Allison Orthner for the gorgeous cover photo www.AllisonOrthner.com

And most importantly…. A very huge thank you to my kids, Alexanna, Cody and Parker, mom and step-dad, Kim, Tim and Abbey; they supported me in ways only a family could. I love you all. Thank you

Kel

Disclaimer: This is a true story, and the characters and events are real. However, in some cases, the names, descriptions, and locations have been changed, and some events have been altered, combined or condensed for storytelling purposes, but the overall chronology is an accurate depiction of the authors' experiences. **You may also be uncomfortable with some of the language and content.**

ISBN 13#: 978-1-9990295-0-0

Cover photo by: Allison Orthner for the gorgeous cover photo www.AllisonOrthner.com
Editing by Liberty Forrest and Patricia Ogilvie
Special thank you to: Chalkboard Media – Chris & Ellen – the two best producers in the world.
Dr. Barry Lycka – for doing laser surgery on me and making my scars more manageable, for free.

FOREWORD

Back in the early 70's, I was a firefighter and my partner and I ended up in a horrible backdraft house fire in Whitecourt, Alberta. My partner suffered with 85% burns to his body while I was burned on 15% of my body.

I remember being in the University of Alberta Hospital and walking by a little girl's room. She was burned quite extensively. She was completely covered in bandages, except for her eyes. She was very heavily medicated because of all the pain she was in from her burns.

I would stop at her room and look in the window and try and make her laugh. All I could see was her big green eyes. She was in isolation so I couldn't visit her, just watch her outside the window.

I remember my doctor, Dr. Shimizu saying to me, "You are lucky, your burns will heal and you will no longer have to come back for more surgery. That little girl over there, will need surgeries for the rest of her life."

I always remembered that little girl with the big eyes and wondered what happened to her. I wish I would have gotten her name, but I didn't. Many times I thought of her and then one day, I went to a community supper and sat with a nice couple.

I told them my story of how I got burnt in the early 70's in the backdraft and spent time in the U of A Hospital. The lady said that her niece Kelly got burnt around that time, maybe she's the little girl he was referring to. I gave her my contact information and asked if she would contact Kelly and see if she's the little burned girl with the big eyes.

Sure enough she was! I was so excited I got to meet Kelly after all those years of wondering what happened to her. She was a trooper then and she's definitely a trooper now! I'm so proud of her and her accomplishments and how she's trying to help people with her story. She is definitely not a quitter in life!

Robert Walker

INTRODUCTION

There's so much beauty in this world and yet some people instead choose to see the bad, the negative and the ugly. They immediately want to see what isn't good enough to them instead of seeing the beauty.

The word 'beauty' or 'beautiful' is such a powerful word. It can either totally destroy a person's self-image or it can enhance it. A lot of women feel they aren't worth anything unless they are beautiful and perfect. If they don't have the perfect body, clothes or make-up then they can't be beautiful and people shouldn't think they are. But they are wrong.

The word 'beauty' sets almost impossible standards for women and girls to live up to. It's almost like the word has an uncontrollable and unknown power over women. Whether you want this word to affect you or not, it does in different ways.

The word is in every aspect of the media throughout the world. No matter how hard you try to ignore it, it's there. I don't understand why people and the media set such impossible standards for beauty. Even when they think they have taken a picture of the most beautiful woman, they still Photoshop it to create a fake, false beauty that doesn't exist.

If only the media would understand women really want to see the real beauty in women, not the fake stuff they create. My purpose with this book is to show people if the (used to be) ugly scar-faced girl can feel beautiful, so can you!

Not only is it so prevalent in the media, but we even have 'beauty' contests to prove one woman is more beautiful than another. And as if that isn't bad enough, we have also 'child' beauty pageants because apparently we need to show children early on in their lives whether they are beautiful or not! Seriously? Are you kidding me?

My definition of real beauty is when you are as natural as you want to be, without having to impress someone else. You are comfortable in your own skin. You do whatever it is that gives YOU your 'wow' factor.

You dress to please YOU rather than somebody else.

You focus on your opinion of YOU and not somebody else's opinion of you.

Ultimately, you dress and look to impress YOU and nobody else. You aren't worried whether someone else thinks you are pretty or beautiful enough.

I will never forget when I was making the decision about whether to get a prosthetic ear to replace my deformed, burned ear.

When I was a kid, I hated my ugly, deformed ear. I wouldn't wear pony tails because I didn't want anyone to see my ugly, deformed ear. As I got older, I realized my ear made me different and I liked it that way. The time I really fell in love with my ear was the day I made my final decision about whether to get a new prosthetic ear or not.

I thought it might be nice to have a 'normal' looking ear. It might help me hear better and maybe when I would wear my hair up people wouldn't stare so much. But when I heard about the surgery it would take to create the new ear and how I would lose my little ear forever, I decided not to make the change.

I asked the doctor how they would make me a prosthetic ear and he said, *"We have you come in for surgery, we cut the old ear off, then drill the titanium posts into your skull, then we make a mold from your other ear and make you a new ear and then you just snap the new ear onto the posts every morning."* And this whole process would take roughly three months to complete.

My next question was *"What if I don't like my new ear and want my old ear back?"* And the doctor said, *"Oh well, it will be gone, there's no way you can get your old ear back."*

That wasn't acceptable to me and I thought why am I doing this? Why am I getting a new ear just so someone else can think I'm beautiful? I don't see my ear as ugly any more. I can't even see my ear unless I look in the mirror and again I asked myself, *'why am I going to put myself through all this pain just so someone else can feel more comfortable with my looks?'*

The new ear wasn't going to help me hear any better – it was purely for cosmetic reasons to get this new ear. Another deciding factor was when my former husband said, *"Kel, I don't want to nibble on a plastic ear, why do you think you need to change your ear, what's wrong with the one you have?"* I just laughed and said *"Okay, no new ear for me, I love my little ear; it's a part of me and I don't want it to change. I don't want to lose my little ear."*

This book was written with two purposes; firstly, to share my 'Still Beautiful' documentary which recreates my life story of getting burned as a two-year-old and following my life until the present as an international speaker, best-selling author, artist and single mom of three teenage kids.

The second purpose (part two) is to share stories from my friends who want to share their life of feeling ugly and how they realized true beauty has nothing to do with what you look like. Your beauty is so much deeper than your skin.

We created three versions of 'Still Beautiful' – a TV broadcast version (48-minutes), feature film version (73-minutes) and Christian versions of both the broadcast and feature film versions. Part One of this book is the transcript from the feature film version of Still Beautiful (which is 73-minutes long) complete with a few pictures directly from the documentary. If you would like to host a movie night with your group, please go to our website www.StillBeautifulDoc.com for more information.

My purpose in life is to show how beauty is so much more than what we look like. In the documentary, I share three lessons I've learned over my life time and if you follow them, I promise you, you will feel 'Still Beautiful'. After the documentary transcript, I go into more details about the three lessons.

Enjoy and please share the book with your friends and family who need more inspiration and truth about being 'Still Beautiful'. And if you know of any organizations who would like to show the 'Still Beautiful' documentary or would like to hire me to speak, please reach out to us and email me at admin@KellyFalardeau.com. We want to reach as many people as possible and remember.... You are Still Beautiful just the way you are.

Hugs, Kelly

PART ONE – STILL BEAUTIFUL
DOCUMENTARY TRANSCRIPT

Kelly in bathroom looking in the mirror, describing her scars and getting ready for the day

 My grandma always used to tell me this story about how she could see little leaves in my face.

I think she was just trying to make me feel better, but uh... I've got all these scars on the side of my face, and especially on my right side, there's lots of scars there, and it goes all the way down across my neck.

And then my ear. It looks like a little deformed ear with no tip on the end of it, so it... it doesn't work very well and I can't hear very good.

And then this scarring around my mouth is quite tight, so it doesn't allow me to open my mouth as wide as some people can.

I'm actually missing a nipple and then the other nipple I have, you know, I sometimes hardly call it a nipple, but it sticks out all the time, so it's kind of funny, and my friend Cindy and I... She's another burn survivor, and her and

I, we were at a burn conference and we started the... the no nip club.

And people would laugh at us 'cause we'd ask all the men and women "Are you members of the no nip club?" We... We just wanted to have fun with it and just celebrate our... our bodies being so different.

And the scars go all the way around my chest to my back, and in the middle of the back is a strip of natural skin and the rest of it is all scars. So yeah, I'm covered in scars. But so what? I'm different and that's what makes me special.

Kelly on 'Power in Me' youth empowerment event - about to speak to 3000 teens

 It's not easy for me to get up on a stage in front of 3,000 kids, but I push myself to do it, because when I was growing up as the ugly scar-faced girl, I wish that I had someone to help me figure out how to love myself.

 MC: Now we are going to have our first speaker. This woman is an amazing display of courage and fight. I often say, it's not what happens to you. It's how you choose to deal with it. And if you need proof of that, please welcome to the stage my friend - the amazing Kelly Falardeau.

 Thank you. Thank you. When I grew up, I had a talking mirror. Not this one, but I had a mirror like this. And that mirror was my enemy. And I wanna share with you how that mirror went from being the enemy in my life, to being my friend. You see, when I got burnt, as a two-year-old, I thought I would be ugly forever. But I became a mom, I became a speaker, I became an advocate, I became a person who just wanted to help other people. And even though I knew the kids were calling me the ugly scar face girl, I am Kelly, and I am still beautiful.

The Tragic Accident

I'm Jean Woodhouse, and I am Kelly's mom. And she was born on July the fourteenth, uh, 1966. Just this little round pink ball, with a little bit of dark hair and the little dark eyes, and the most beautiful thing I have ever seen in my life, and wow. It was phenomenal. I just remember being happy.

After I was born, we moved to my grandparents' farm. Mom stayed at home with me, while Dad worked at his day job in the city.

Otherwise, life in the country was great. It was a tight-knit community with people stopping by at all times.

I'm Willy deJong, I was a neighbour of Kelly and the parents and the grandparents. We, uh, curled together and I guess we could say we drank together, and, uh, we were all good friends.

Everything was so-called perfect in my life, and that was the last time. Because when Kelly had her accident, that was devastating.

All right. Let's do it!

I was two-years-old that day, when my grandfather asked my two cousins to burn some old shingles.

Cousin Mike: I bet you can't throw them from all the way back here.

Cousin Rod: Yes I can.

I don't remember the date - all I know is it was the end of August. And it was a beautiful sunny day and my dad had taken the shingles off of his garage and, uh, had new ones put on. And, you know, I'm 19, and I'm six months pregnant, I'm making supper, my husband's going to the boxing club and he's working out, so he's gonna be late, and my dad and mom had gone off to a barbecue, and, you know, we've never had an accident on the farm.

My cousins kept throwing shingles into the fire, and like any two-year-old, I wanted to join in.

I came down there for a visit, or come to borrow something, and there was two boys and they were playing with the fire. And the burning barrel was just a-givin' 'er.

That's when a spark flew out.

And all of a sudden I see this flame...
Oh my god Kelly, Kelly!

All of a sudden I can hear this commotion going on outside, I can s-- hear screaming and yelling, and what the heck is going on? And that's when I see Kelly coming from around the barrel... and her clothes are on fire.

I didn't know what to do. So I grabbed her and I rolled her in the dirt. And just couldn't believe it was happening.

Kelly!

COUSINS: Auntie Jean, Auntie Jean!

And I go running out there. The top of her pants are still on fire and I put my hand over that.

She picked up Kelly and she was frustrated, and I was frustrated, and in the meantime, let's get in the truck and go bring her to the hospital. She cried and cried and cried. And you couldn't blame the poor girl, because she had polyester clothes stuck to her skin.

She said, "Mummy, it hurts." *(crying)* I felt so helpless. Terrified.

Kelly and her mom arriving in Emergency at Hospital

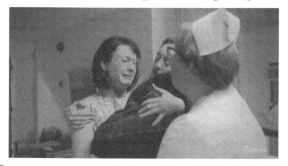

 My mom was in tears as she ran in with me.

 As soon as we hit the emergency ward of the old... the university hospital, she was scooped up, and taken to the operating room, and they put a cut down into her neck, one into her groin and one into her ankle, where they're running saline solution into her.

They did a tracheotomy on her, so that she could breathe. They... opened up her right arm, cause it was going to burst, it was burnt all the way around, and her chest, and her left arm, her face, a little bit on the back of her head, and the insides of her knees.

So the only thing that saved her from her burns not being more extensive was the wet diaper that I left on her.

And in the waiting time, I was bargaining with God: "Please let this be a dream. This can't be true. What have I done? Am I this bad of a sinner that this is my punishment? Don't punish some... an innocent child."

And I remember Dr. Shimizu coming in around eleven o'clock. I said to him, "What are her chances?" And he said, "50/50." And all I could see was... somebody flipping a coin saying, "Heads you win, tails you lose." I'll never forget that as long as I live. Just... wow. Those aren't very good odds.

My husband, Bill, finally found me in the hospital, and it was... horrible. Horrible. You can bargain all you want, but there's no going back. There's nothing you can do to change this.

Kelly at Rachel's hair salon

 Okay, so what are we doing today?

 What are we doing? The usual - make me look good!

 Okay, are we going to have bangs, are we growing them out? What are we doing?

 I don't know. I don't know. I kind of like... I think I like the bangs. I don't know.

 But just a little bit shorter.

 But don't forget about the bald spot.

 Yep, absolutely. Okay, so let's wash you up then. So how are the kids, how's everybody?

 The kids are great. Alex graduated this year.

 I know, when I still think she's kindergarten, *(laughs)* right?

 Now she can go to the bar even.

Not without us! *(laughs)*

 I'm Rachel Gour. I met Kelly when we were fifteen, in grade ten, in Spruce Grove, at high school, um... the most trying time of our years, *(laughs) b*ecoming young adults. And to me she was always just Kelly and has always been just Kelly. Once she's in my chair we get into very candid conversations about, "Okay, so this is what's going on, and what do you think?" We analyze everything.

 I have a question.

 What?

 Have you decided what you're doing?

 About what?

 About laser treatments?

 Well, I don't know it's, um... For four years now I've been trying to figure, do I want to do my face or not.

 Right?

 Because when I was growing up, I categorized everybody under two categories: you were either an ugly person or you were a beautiful person, right? And so I believed that I represented the ugly people.

 Come on.

 Well, when you... when you grow up as the ugly scarface girl, that's... the truth of it is.

 But you know, to me, you've been my pretty Kelly.

I know.

 And it makes me crazy that you would think that way.

 Well of course, but that's... the truth of it is...

 It's... I get it. I do get it.

 Everybody hates the word ugly, but I'm used to it.

 Yeah.

 It doesn't bother me like it bothers a lot of people, and if I go and get my face done, then maybe I can't be in that group anymore. And we've talked about this many times and you're like "No, I don't want you to change your face."

 I just don't know if I want you to. Like I don't... I want you to do it if you want to feel good about it. If it makes you feel good, of course I want you to do it. Like, for how many years did I never see your scars, and didn't even think that they altered anything, until that time with the twins.

 When I was pregnant with the twins, and my scars were so tight, eventually they did start to... to bleed.

 Yes.

 They were splitting and they were bleeding. And so the scars were starting to get really tight, and, um... causing me some pain.

 Yeah.

So that was one of the reasons I decided to go for the laser, was to alleviate some of that tightness.

 Which I supported all the way through, because I saw you in those moments before those babies came.

 Yeah, exactly.

 Of course you had to have big babies.

 I know. *(laughs)*

Meet the family time - Kelly cooking breakfast for her kids, Alexanna, Cody and Parker

 So, Cody, you want some pancakes for breakfast today?

 Yeah, I'm hungry.

 Yeah, yeah, yeah.

 Oh man, that cat's so cute.

 He's so cute. Mom, look at him.

Awww. Cody, you want to flip the pancakes again please?

I am a single mother. I have three kids. My daughter is eighteen, Alex. And then I have twin boys, Cody and Parker, and they are fourteen.

You think they're ready?

Yeah, think that looks good?

Yeah, I think so.

Definitely being a single mom is challenging. Especially because I'm the kind of mom with a mission. I'm balancing my business, I'm a bestselling author, a motivational speaker, a painter, an artist. So definitely a lot on the go, and my day is planned.

Okay guys, summer. We gotta talk about summer plans. We've got paint night coming up next week. So next Tuesday we're going to the tea place in Edmonton.

What day is next Tuesday, though?

Next Tuesday. *(laughs)*

Oh, okay.

You goof.

I love it, you know, love being busy. In fact, when I'm not busy that's when I get a little depressed or upset or, you know, I just feel bored.

So, Cody and Parker, you guys are going back to Dad's tonight. Cause I'm leaving for San Francisco tomorrow. 'Kay, so you guys will be with Dad for that whole time. And Alex, you...

I feel like I do well as a mom, and then there's other times I feel like I'm just, you know, a horrible mom, because of the travelling that I do, and because I'm so focused on my career, and things that I want to accomplish, and yet I feel like I can't always be there for my kids.

I've had many conversations with my kids about it, and Cody says, "Well Mom, it's your passion, you love it, why wouldn't you do it?"

Kelly packing for her business trip to San Francisco

 Hey Buzzy! {Buzzy is the superstar family cat} How are you, Buzz? You going to come to San Francisco with me? No?

I always pack a few of these blankets when I go to a speaking event. They're for my charity, Blankets for Burn Kids. And people often wanna buy one or two after my talks. And in San Francisco, I'll be speaking at a Women's Conference. But what I'm most excited about is seeing my old friend Cindy.

Cindy and I met when I was, like, 21-years-old, and she was the very first female woman burn survivor that I had met. So I'm so excited about seeing her, because we've been able to have those deep conversations about beauty. And if we've ever wondered how we would feel if we were scar-less, or if we feel beautiful now, even with our scars. And both of us are now divorced, so this is gonna be another really interesting conversation, because my ex-husband told me that, you know, good possibility that some other men wouldn't want me, because I am scarred.

Kelly in her bedroom discussing her divorce

When I got married, things seemed perfect. I had a spouse who I thought loved me, scars and all. But every honeymoon eventually ends.

I was, you know, a stay-at-home mom, I had a part-time job, and, yeah I was married, and, yeah, I had the kids, but I wasn't happy. And I had to start making some changes, and start realizing that the self-love doesn't just come from, you know, the outside. It comes from what you're doing. And decided I was going to share my message of who I was and... and just be that authentic person that people can relate to.

I was changing and growing, but my marriage wasn't.

He didn't see the value that my story had, and how it could impact other people. He saw me as being a mom, you know? The frumpy housewife mom who didn't... who wasn't successful.

And I realized that I had to put me first. And my truth was that I wasn't happy. I wasn't happy with my job and I wasn't happy with my marriage.

And I realized the only way to be happy is to end both of them. And, uh, within six months I ended my job and my marriage. So it was major, major transformation.

Can't forget my toothbrush and my brush, so, we'll put that in here.

I believe it's very important for me to share my story. It gives me that whole sense of purpose. Everywhere that I travel, it's about helping all of us to understand that our beauty doesn't come from what we look like. Because so many people are so focused on having the perfect hair or having the perfect clothes or having the perfect, you know, flawless skin, and the beauty doesn't come from that.

ANNOUNCER: Welcome to San Francisco, ladies and gentlemen.

Kelly Arrived in San Francisco

You know, it comes from our heart and our souls. And this is my heart and soul, being able to share my message with others around the world.

When I was thirteen I remember having a conversation with my mom. And I said, I'm the only one in the world who's burnt. And she goes, "No, you're not." And I said, "Okay, I'm the only one in Canada who's burnt." "No, you're not." And I said, "Okay, I'm the only one in Alberta who's burnt." And she said, "No, you're not." And I said, "Okay, fine, I'm the only one in Edmonton who's burnt." And she said, "Well, maybe."

And I know she said that just, you know, to shut me up, but it truly felt that way. Because we didn't have Instagram. We didn't have Snapchat. We didn't have those ways of connecting. And so I grew up believing that I was the only one in the world who was burnt.

I was always concerned about, you know, being stared at. And I was always trying to figure out, "What are they thinking?" And I wish that I would have had the internet when I was younger, so that I could have could have found other burn survivors like me and be able to connect with them and realize that I'm not the only one out there.

For years, I had no one in my life who truly understood what I was going through. That's until I met my friend Cindy.

Kelly meeting her friend Cindy Rutter in San Francisco

 My name is Cindy Rutter. I, um, am also a burn survivor. I was in a house explosion in 1959 and sustained a burn injury over eighty-five percent of my body. And back in 1959, burn technology was very different - uh, they basically said there was no way that I was gonna live. But I had people that were totally committed to keeping me alive at the time. And hence, here I am.

 Good to see you.

 I know. It's been forever.

 So, how are you?

 I don't know, life's been crazy. I left my husband.

 Yeah? And is your life better?

 Well, I think it's better to be single and lonely than married and lonely.

 Yeah. Oh, I agree. I completely agree.

Growing up with a severe burn injury, there were a lot of obstacles. People staring, making fun of you. The, um, inability, really, to say, hey, you know, this is what happened to me. Because kids don't really care, they're... kids are bullies, they were bullies then and they're bullies now.

I believe that part of my strength and, um, inner resiliency, if you will, came from the incredible family support that I had. It was, you're capable of doing anything anyone else can, and hold your head high, and be proud of who you are.

But I do believe there are differences between male and female burn survivors. Like, I hear a lot of the young males that will say, well, the scars make them macho, and it's, um... okay that they've got scars. Whereas our society is so focused on females being flawless that, um, when you're a woman with scars, it's a lot different, and so you need the support to believe that it's okay to look physically different We do... I mean, that's the reality. We do look physically different. We have scars on our bodies. And they're not gonna go away.

And, so how do we help people understand that in spite of the fact that they may look physically different, that doesn't define who they are as human beings?

Kelly speaking at a Women's event in San Francisco

Thank you. You know, I was married to the same man for twenty-four years. And I ended up, um, wondering why, after about a year and a half {after my divorce}, I wasn't being asked out on dates.

So I decided to do the online dating thing. First guy I talked to says, "Nope, sorry, your scars would bother me, I can't go out with you." And I'm thinking, "Okay, one down, one million nine hundred ninety-nine thousand nine hundred and ninety-nine to go. I'm good.

And then I end up, uh, talking to the second guy, He sends me a text message, and it said, "Do you like to kiss?" Okay, now, I am smart enough to know I have to... a kiss means something.

And I go, "Yeah, I do, but I kind of like to get to know the guy a few times before I decide if I wanna do that or not." He says, "You know you're no beauty queen, right?"

And I thought, what the heck? Why is this man talking this way? Like, you wanna get into my pants and you tell me I'm no beauty queen. And I get it, I am no beauty queen. But I don't have to be. I don't have to be a beauty queen in order to be loved, in order to be good enough.

How many times do we do that? We think we're not beautiful enough, we're not perfect enough, we think that we're not making enough money, we're don't have the best car. We don't have the right makeup.

And I've felt that way many of times. There's many times I'd walk in the room and I would just crumble. Because I felt like I wasn't beautiful enough, I wasn't smart enough, I wasn't successful enough.
And I don't want anybody to ever feel like they're ugly, or like they're unwanted, or that they're unneeded in this life. Every single person in this room is more than enough. And you deserve to be loved, you deserve to be needed, you deserve to be wanted.

Kelly, that was so fabulous, I haven't heard you speak like that, and... we need to celebrate.

We need to celebrate.

How about a glass of wine, at a winery. Fifteen minutes away.

We don't stop at one. We don't get to stop at one, okay?

Two, three?

 Maybe four.

 Okay, let's go.

 We're going to call Uber.

 There we go, Uber.

 Uber's taking us home.

 Bring us home, Uber.

Kelly and Cindy at Picchetti Winery in San Francisco

 Hi.

 Hello, good afternoon, thanks for joining us today. Here at the Picchetti, we let you build your own wine-tasting flight, but don't feel like you have to choose them all at once.

 Okay.

 But if we want them all?

(laughs) Bring it on! I like where your head's at. Let's celebrate with some sparkling wine, and then we'll get the show on the road from there.

Okay. Ooh, I like that.

Sauvignon Blanc here.

Cheers.

Can you taste, like, woody taste in white wines?

What a perfect time to ask! I'm going to pour different wines for you, and it's... I'm gonna give you enough so you can share, so you can appreciate how that same grape goes in two different directions and notice a difference, or not.

So crisp and young...

Right.

Old and aged.

Exactly right.

It's appropriate. If you take the crisp, I'll take the aged. I mean, come on!

Cheers. Here's to youngness! Don't drink it all.
(laughter)

I'm really humbled that Kelly says that she's learned a lot from me. But I also have learned a lot from Kelly. I think she's got determination, perseverance. She inspires me. She has a gift to give to people, and that gift is by sharing her own personal experience, her personal story. She has made a difference not only in my life, but in lots of people's lives.

Carmen (mom) and Taylor (daughter) chatting about Taylor's letters

 So, why did you write this one?

 I don't know.

 What's it about?

 Drugs. And dying. Yeah.

 And so why do you want to burn it?

 My name is Taylor. I'm 19-years-old. I met Kelly about two years ago when my mom gave me Kelly's book, 'Self-Esteem Doesn't Come in a Bottle', because I had been self-harming, and struggling with anxiety and depression.

 So it says you can't breathe, and that you are a failure. Is that what you think?

 Yeah.

 Now or then?

 Then.

And then after you wrote it?

 I felt better because I was like, I don't feel that way anymore, like, I'm glad I don't.

 So you got it out, it's over?

 Yeah.

 So are you ready to get rid of it?

 Yeah.

 So,, put it in the fire.

 I was always a really awkward child. I never fit in, I never really made friends that easy. I had ADHD, which obviously didn't help with, you know, school, and so I felt odd, and I felt out, because I felt like I wasn't pretty enough, that I wasn't skinny enough. And I felt more alone than anything. And then everything just kind of hit after that, and, um, I became more and more depressed. Which unfortunately led to anxiety. And I was, uh, cutting myself. Like, the pain was gone for only, maybe, a few minutes. But it wasn't for attention or it wasn't an addiction, it was my depression and... and feeling like I was alone, I felt like I needed the release.

The day that my mother brought Kelly's book, my mom said, "Here. You need to read this." And so I was kind of hesitant towards it. I was like, "Uh, I don't know. I don't... I don't think so. Maybe not yet." And, um... And then I finally got over my stubbornness and I was like, "Ah, okay."

 And I think that was a big thing for me, just because she was able to compare her getting burned to having self-esteem and feeling good about herself. And she comes out stronger than anybody I've ever known.

Paint Nite at the Tea House Café in Edmonton

 I'm hosting a paint night at the Tea House Cafe in Edmonton.

I just started painting two years ago. I don't really have any trained skills in being a painter. It's all just by listening to my heart and just doing it.

So I have a couple rules. And one of the rules is, no fun allowed. No, we can have fun. We gotta have fun, right? I mean, painting's all about fun!

Uh, the second rule I have is, no perfection allowed. Perfection holds you back, it makes you be critical of your life, and I don't want anything to hold you back, because everybody has their own... their own expression in life.

So, the message tonight is this: we are gonna create this masterpiece that has a giraffe on it, and you get to make it whatever colours you want.

Who's ready to start painting? *(cheering)* Awesome.

 Too many people think that they have to be perfect in their lives. And so that's one of my rules. You don't get to be a perfectionist. Because people need to stop being so hard on themselves. And they need to start doing things that make them happy.

How you doing, Jen? Hey, that looks good. You're doing awesome. How about you? Cool, good! Everybody's giraffes have so much character.

 Well, look who's here. Miss Taylor!

Hi, guys.

Miss Taylor, how are you?

 I'm good.

 Come on up here, gorgeous. Give me a hug. So good to see you.

 So good to see you. Where would you like me to sit?

 I think you're sitting back there, with Alex?

 Back there with Alex?

 Yeah, go check out Alex.

 That painting is definitely awesome. I see a lot of blue.

 It's abstract.

 It's like a Picasso!

 Yeah.

 Okay, so, whose painting turned out perfect? *(laughter)* Okay, so whose painting didn't turn out perfect? I know, right? But you guys all had something different, something that's unique, something that represents you. Let's just be our authentic real selves, because that's who we're meant to be.

 So thank you everybody for joining us tonight. Feel free to keep painting and finish up your painting, and yeah, thank you. Thank you for being here.

Thank you.

 Kelly really changed my perspective on life. I think mainly just hearing how she got over her scars, and how I could get over mine. And she just kind of made me open my eyes to see that I was better than my cutting and my eating disorder, all that kind of stuff. She made me realize that I could be somebody a lot better, somebody I was proud of.

Kelly and Taylor chatting about their scars at Kelly's car

 Hey, I need a hand taking the art supplies and blankets out to my car. Can you help me?

 Sure.

 Okay, gra-- great.

 Taylor did a lot of self-harming, and so many kids are self harming and they're thinking it's okay, but they don't have strategies to learn how to quit. And they don't know-- have strategies on coping with stress, and how to stand out in a positive way.

 Here you go.

 So, have a seat. I know there's times when you are outraged at how people treat you. And, uh, it's sad sometimes when we're on the bus.

 Yeah.

...and people are looking at our scars. And they're judging us. I remember a time when I went to a garage sale. As I was walking around, this lady took a look at me and she noticed my scars on my face and my body. And she says to me, "They couldn't do better than that?" And I was shocked. I was outraged. I was upset, because she didn't know about everything I had been through.

And normally I would be the bitch, really that was how I used to handle things. I would be the bitch. I'd be like, "Who are you? Like, screw off." But I said to her, "I happen to think I look pretty damn good." And I turned around and I walked away.

I know you've got some scars that you don't like showing, but those scars are here so that you can teach other girls, okay? That's why you went through what you did. And I know it was tragic, but you're still here. Become a speaker, become an author, do whatever it takes, and don't let anybody stop you from what you want in your life.

And I know it's hard. It's hard when you get on the bus, and when you walk down the street and people are staring at you. I get it. But don't be ashamed of your scars. Cause you're a beautiful girl.

Thank you.

Okay?

Nurse and porter bringing Kelly into hospital room when she was a teenager

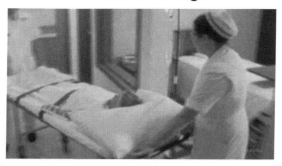

 By the time I was twenty-one, I had over forty procedures on my burns and scars.

 So I spent a lot of my time in the hospital. Every second summer would be in the hospital a whole month, because back in those days they didn't do day surgeries.

So yeah, it was devastating having to spend my summer in the hospital instead of being able to run around and play, and... with my cousins or my friends. You know, it's just not fun when you are wrapped in bandages.

So, yeah, I felt very isolated. It felt like I had my own separate world. And every single time I would have a surgery, we'd be wondering, is this gonna work?

So definitely my childhood was challenging, because I was not only dealing with my burns, and having to be in the hospital a lot, but I was also dealing with school life.

Kelly and kids at school in grade five

TEACHER: Right, so you're multiplying the numbers... doesn't matter which order...

Grade five was a very challenging year. Grade five was when I walked past my teacher's desk and I saw this picture - it was a circle - eyes, nose and mouth - and it had scribbles all over it, and it said, "Scarface".

And I wasn't supposed to see it, but I did. And it confirmed to me what the kids thought of me, that I was the scarface girl.

Kelly being bullied by kids at school in grade five

And then there was Joey. Every day we would have lunch together. His mom bought cookies and my mom made cookies, so he always wanted to eat my cookies instead.

And anyways, he, um... he decided that he was gonna hang out with the bully. And he came up to me and said, "Kelly, I don't want to be your friend anymore." And that was the last time we talked.

And those hurtful things that people would say would affect me probably more so than the physical because you replay those situations over and over and over.

I don't wanna see you anymore, I don't even wanna talk to you.

I tried to teach her that it didn't matter what other people said. But words hurt worse than a punch in the face. I know I experienced both, and I'd rather have the punch in the face. Cause that goes away. But the words you don't forget.

I don't wanna see you anymore, I don't even wanna talk to you.

She doesn't realize how beautiful she was. And beauty is skin deep, ugly is straight to the bone. And Kelly's not ugly. In any way shape or form. But she's devastated, because "now I'm going to be this way for the rest of my life". I know that's what she's thinking.

 All I wanted was for someone to say, "You're beautiful." And, you know, there was times when I wonder, "Why do I want to live?" And I didn't want to live. So I would pray to end my life.

Kelly and Tina, (her laser technician) at Dr Lycka's office getting ready for laser surgery

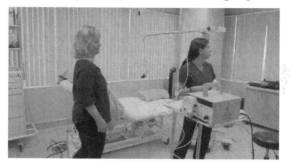

 Hey Kelly, we're ready for you. How are you doing?

 I'm good, thanks.

 Come on back.

 Okay.

 I am here today to see Dr. Barry Lycka, who's my laser surgeon, and I am a little bit nervous about today, because I decided to get some laser done on my face.

 So I'll get you to change into a robe, I'm gonna grab one for you, and then we're gonna get started.

 Okay. Okay, sounds good. It's, um, very challenging for me to make that decision. Because it felt like I was changing my identity. I feel like I am betraying my people. And so today is especially hard.

So I'm just gonna kind of feel around and just make some markings. So what I'm gonna do is give you a mirror, so you can just kind of look.

I told Dr Lycka when he approached me about doing laser surgery that he could do anything he wanted, except for my face. But, when I was a teenager, that was my dream, was to be scar-less. But the doctors couldn't make that happen, back in the sixties, and the seventies, and the eighties, when I was going through my surgeries. But now we have the technology to make that happen. And so even though it's an emotional thing for me, I believe that I am ready to make that change.

Three, two one. Is that Okay?

Yep, I didn't feel nothing.

Good. So I'm just gonna go - let me know if you're feeling anything…

The purpose of laser surgery is, when you have extensive scarring like I have, your skin gets very tight. And the scarring will hold your skin in places that you don't necessarily want it to be, and it... and it contracts, and it makes it really difficult to have some movement.

That looks beautiful. That looks... you gonna go through an amazing process here in the next couple of days.

I'm Dr. Barry Lycka. I'm a dermatologist here in Edmonton, Alberta, Canada.

So what we are doing with scarring now, is we're turning back the healing process. We're turning back the process the body uses to heal the scar. See, a scar is a very bad thing. The body fixes something, but it has to fix it quickly, so it does it wrongly.

Now, those scars start to grow with time. They start to act like a girdle on a person if they're on the body. They act like an external coat of armour, so a person can't move. They can't use their body in the way it has to be used.

With our new advanced scar technology, we can actually turn it back to normal. We can make it much better for people. And I think Kelly Falardeau is a prime example of that. She's going to be able to move her face more, she's going to be able to move her neck more, she's going to be able to get a full range of motion for the first time in years, and at the end of the day that's gonna be a nicer, brighter person. But she's gonna go through an emotional flooding for a few days. She's gonna go through crying, she's gonna go through tearing - a lot of people actually relive the injury that they had, and that's a hard thing for them. So it is very important that the results are very, very subtle.

David, Kelly's friend arrives to take her home from laser surgery

 You okay?

 Hey!

 I've been waiting for you and I don't know how to hug you without hurting you...

 I know, we always like big hugs.

 You okay?

 Yep, I am. This time I thought it would be really nice to have a somebody with me, so I brought, um, a really good friend of mine - David.

Let's get out of here.

 Thank you.

 David is special because he gets it. He, uh, understands the deep emotional issues that people can have. And he's very supportive of that.

Kelly and David chatting about doing laser surgery on her face

 Here we go, I've got some peppermint tea for us.. Good to be back, right? Back at home, after that…

 Yeah.

 How does the bandage feel?

 The bandage feels good.

 Cause it's, like, ear to ear, that's a lot of bandage.

 I know, yeah, it looks like I have a Santa Claus beard on..

 Kind of, yeah.

It does. But, um, but that's okay. It... It looks painful but it's not. So tomorrow I will be back to normal, being able to do everything that I...

 So let me ask you, then, so why today did you choose to do your face for the first time?

 You're asking me the tough questions, aren't you!

 But I've known you for so long, I love the concept of your inner beauty and what that means. So in your conversation in your mind, what shifted?

 I don't... I don't know if there was actually one moment.

 Okay, so rather than one moment, can you kind of track an evolution of what would make you be more open to doing that?

 Well, I honestly believe that I was supposed to get burnt, so that I could learn all of the lessons, so that I could go through being stared at, and teased, and rejected, and shunned so that I have this knowledge to teach others. So yeah, it was very challenging for me to decide, "Okay, I'm going to do my face!"

 Yeah.

 Right, it was, for four years, it was like, "Am I gonna do my face?" - "I don't know." - "Am I gonna do my face?" - "I don't know." Like, there's all these "I don't knows".

 Well, **because** initially you said you didn't want to, right?

 I didn't want to.

 Yeah. Was that a bit of a defiance? Like, "I don't need to do my face cause I am beautiful and I know that"?

 Yeah, I mean, that was one of the reasons I decided not to do it.

Initially. The kind of defiance, "I don't have to."

 Initially, was because I'm fine. What's wrong with me? I'm beautiful the way I am, and so if some man wants me, he's going to have to learn to love me like this.

 Of course, I mean, that's...

 Either you love this, or you don't get this.

 So what changed in you? To make you say, "Hey, I'm ready to do that."

 Well, sometimes I'm just tired of being stared at.

 Still.

 Still. It's just hard sometimes, I'm walking down the mall and everybody's staring at me. Just... Just tired. Just tired of trying to be strong. You know, and tired of, you know, pretending I'm not noticing that people are taking second and third looks, you know, they're... going to a swimming pool someone staring at me with their mouth open. And it's like, seriously? Like... Still?

 Yeah. Yeah.

 You know, I just... sometimes I'm tired of being a strong person.

 Yeah, I get it.

 It's not easy for me to walk out the door the way I am. You know, my breasts are too low, my one little partial nipple sticks out, and I can't change that, I can't change that I'm covered in scars, and... but the scars on my chest are way uglier than what's on my face. I just wanna see.

Yeah.

 Is this something that I'm gonna be happy with. It's not a decision that I discussed with anybody else – in fact, I didn't tell any of my closest friends, because I didn't want anybody else's opinion. Right? I wanted this to be a decision that I made, based on me. And I think I finally gave myself permission to make the change, if I wanted it.

Kelly taking off the bandages

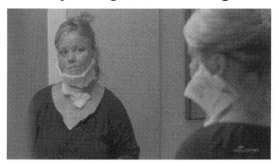

 Taking off the bandages is always a bit scary. It looks like a massive, horrible, painful sunburn. But then they heal, and the scarring becomes less.

There's a word that I absolutely used to hate, and it's called "selfish". Because my mom used to say to me what I was a kid that I was selfish.

And to me it was a very negative word, because it also meant that the only thing that I was doing was thinking of myself, and that I didn't care about other people's feelings.

So it has been very hard for me to shift into realizing that being selfish was a form of self-care. And so for me, it's about, okay, so what can I do? How can I help myself?

It doesn't matter how much laser surgery I do, it doesn't matter how much plastic surgery I do. My scars aren't going to go away. If I can't change this, what can I change?

And I can change my thoughts. I can have people in my life who are going to encourage me, and who are going to empower me, and I can be with people who are going to help me follow my dreams and get me to the places that I want to go, and I can help them, and that's amazing. Because when I am doing something that I love, I am empowered, and I get this incredible energy, and then this energy is what keeps me moving forward.

Kamp Kiwanis

KID: Ring the bell! Ring the bell!

JOSH: Hello, hello. Welcome to camp!

 This is Kamp Kiwanis. It's a sanctuary for underprivileged youth, and it's a place where they can go and just be kids. For three months, twenty-five people helped raise enough money to give each of these kids a special blanket. And as a reward, all the fundraisers will get to skydive with me at the end of the summer, which I've always been terrified of doing, but I'm excited to try.

Kelly speaking to kids at Kamp Kiwanis

JOSH: Alrighty, guys. Let's give it up for Kelly.

 Thank you for having me here. It's such an honour to be able to come to your camp, because I think camp is incredible time. Because when I was growing up as a burn survivor, I didn't know anybody like me.

So I remember being in Grade 4 and 5, and I remember being teased and bullied. And I know that, you know, most of you are not burnt here, but every single person here has something that makes them different, it makes you special and it makes you unique. And I want you to celebrate those differences instead of hiding them.

So on this blanket, this is my original painting and it says 'You are loved. You are needed. You are wanted.' Because I know sometimes we just need something a little bit special to help us feel loved. And that's what's so special about these blankets. These blankets represent love. And so we've got one for everybody. How sweet is that, right? Isn't that cool? Woo-hoo!

 I didn't bring a blanket, so this is perfect.

You didn't bring a blanket? Oh, my gosh. Come on up.

Thank you so much!

You are very welcome. Very, very welcome. Hang on. I gotta wrap it around you.

The reason it's so important to advocate for people who might be different is because there is so much negative stuff that goes on in the world. And especially with social media. Social media today is bombarding teenagers, and women and people in general with all of these negative messages, and it makes them feel like they aren't good enough.

You know, when we were kids, we would get teased or bullied at school, but then we went home and we could almost have, like, a whole separate life. Whereas nowadays, kids feel like they have to be so connected that they're getting bullied twenty-four hours a day.

And it makes me think about how brave Taylor is. She went through a lot in high school, but she's rising above it.

In high school, just everything was difficult. You were judged by what you wore, who you spent your time with, uh... what you did, um... what you ate. And unfortunately, it does affect not just girls but boys as well. And I know that I've had my fair share of somebody posting something about me. Um... They made lies about my mental health. Um... When I first started self-harming, they said I was doing it for attention. And I feel like what would've changed things would be somebody really reaching out a hand, saying, "Are you okay? Do you need help? Do you need to talk?"

And I've thought about this for a while, and I've thought about, um... becoming the advocate for, um... mental health awareness. But I wasn't strong enough, and I feel like now I am. And so... I'm excited to learn from Kelly more about speaking and more about, um... you know, having that confidence to be able to share my story in front of a whole bunch of people.

Kelly and Taylor at coffee shop chatting about Taylor's upcoming speech

 You all ready?

 Yup. I'm ready.

 You ready?

 I'm ready.

 Okay, so one... What we have to do is we have to find a title for you, that an event planner is gonna say "Oh, my gosh. We need to have her." Okay? So one of the things that in your speech, you talk about the self-harming.

 Mm-hmm.

 So you're pretty open with sharing that with people.

 Mm-hmm. Yeah.

 Okay, so a lot of parents are hearing about either their children, or somebody else's children that are harming themselves, and a lot of parents are very scared, and they're not sure what to do, and they're not sure how to get their daughter or their son to stop. So that's what I believe you're a huge advocate for, is to help moms to recognize whether their teenager is harming themself, and how to approach them so that they can get them to stop.

I'm just concerned that I'm gonna mess it up and I'll be super nervous on stage. *(laughs)*

 You know what? The great thing about you're young, and the teens are gonna relate to you very easily.

 I hope so.

 They will. They absolutely will, so that's certainly not a problem. And remember, nobody knows your story like you do, okay?

 Mm-hmm.

 So that's the key thing. And then what we want you to do is to then give the teens steps that they can follow.

 Okay.

On how to change their life. So what are some tips and tricks that we can get people to do to stop self-harming?

 Well, I know that writing and music and all that kind of stuff, um... sports, being active...

 Okay, what else? What other cool things?

 Um... Well, I mean that for me, I like getting tattoos, so, I mean, that's kind of a positive thing, cause you're not harming yourself.

 No, you're just letting somebody else do it.

 (laughs) But it's a tattoo! It's different.

 Did you get some tattoos?

 Mm-hmm. I have a few.

Oh, my gosh. Did you?

 Yeah, I have my arm, my back. I have one on my neck.

 Did you? Okay, so did you get tattoos on your arms?

 Yeah.

 Okay, so what did you do?

 Yeah, so I have the pencil that, uh... my cousin Rhiannon drew. And then I have this stand tall giraffe.

 Aww.

 That was the giraffe I got from my one year clean.

 Oh, wow.

 Yeah. *(laughs)*

 That's exciting. How many years have you been clean now?

 I think we're coming across two.

 Two? That's exciting.

 Two. Yeah.

 Good for you. Okay, and on your left arm?

 Me and my sister are gonna get a tattoo.

Sisters. I know Alex has asked me to get a tattoo, and what she wants is, um... "I love you".

 Aww.

 I've never wanted to get a tattoo, and... But she's asked me about that, and I'm like yeah, we can do a tattoo about that.

 I love it. When I got, um, the script on my back with my mom, it was just so... I felt so more... so much more connected to her, you know?

 Do you?

 Mm-hmm.

 And what does the script on the back say?

 It says I'll love you forever, as long as I'm living.

 Aww.

 It's that Robert Munsch book.

 Aww, that's so sweet.

 And she has, "I'll like you for always, as long as, uh... my baby you'll be" or something like that.

 Aww, that's so cute.

 Yeah.

Taylor and her mom Carmen chatting about their relationship

My relationship with my mom is so unique and so awkward at the same time, but it's so awesome how close we are. It's my mom who has been there through everything, and who has been, you know, my biggest support, and... I don't know how I could have done it without her.

Having a child that self harms is devastating. The first place you go is, "I'm a terrible mom. How come... how come I couldn't stop this? How come I couldn't support her enough that she wouldn't want to do this?"

The fact that she had cut, and you were in the next room. Or coming home and her telling me a story about somebody on the bus told her, you know, she was a terrible person for... for cutting herself, and it's just... it's devastating to... heartbreaking.
Um...

A mom, a dad, can always say, "You're smart and you're beautiful," and I think kids automatically think, you know, "Parents don't know what they're talking about." But when it comes from that... from a different person, it's suddenly believable. And so I think once Taylor and Kelly really started having conversations and, um, and meeting, right, whether it's on facebook or meeting in person and-- and talking about... um... Taylor being beautiful and gorgeous, no matter what, really started to see her believe it. And I think she's really come to... to grips with, "This is something I've done, this is why I did it," but when you have challenges, they... they can make you a stronger person, they can make you... more thoughtful about others. And... that's what we have now.

Taylor and Kelly at the Stony Plain Library – Taylor will be doing her first speech to a group of teens, moms and grandmothers

 So I'm headed to the (Stony Plain) Library. I'm gonna do my speech today. A little bit nervous, but I have time to practice in the car, and I am praying that I am ready. (laughs)

 I think she'll do really well. You know, it's always nerve-wracking to... to get up in front of a crowd, whether it's three or three hundred, right, and so I wouldn't expect her to not be nervous, but I think, as soon as she starts, right, two sentences in, I think she... she'll be gold. She'll rock it.

 So I want to welcome everybody here to the Stony Plain Library. It's so cool to see you all here. So I've been mentoring Taylor, and Taylor's got an amazing background. So I've invited Taylor to come and share her stories, so that she can help the teenagers overcome some of those challenges too. Okay, Taylor! Take it away.

 Awesome. Hey so, hi, I'm Taylor. Uh, like Kelly said, I'm nineteen-years-old. I was self-harmer, uh, when I was 12-years-old - that's when it all kind of went down, junior high. And I still struggle with anxiety, I'm not gonna lie. I'm not perfect, nobody is. I still struggle with depression. So I'm gonna give you some tips on how to help, um...

 For my first speech, I didn't expect that many people, uh, probably just because I was doubting everything, um... but it was really nice to see all the different ages – we had a grandmother, and then we had some girls... I wasn't expecting that many teenagers, and I think that was a really nice refresher for me. *(laughs)*

I've kind of been going over my steps - I've been to therapy, I take medication - I'm not ashamed, cause... no stigma, um, and I also still talk to my mother, who is, like, the best person to talk to. Cause they know who you are. They love you with all of their heart - talking to the teens here, cause we don't believe it. Do we? No? *(laughs)* I know that my mom...

Kelly told me to speak from the heart, really just talk about... what I'm feeling at that moment, because then people will relate a lot more.

Friends will come and go. Some people will stay for a year, some people will stay for a couple months. The people who are there through thick and thin are the people who are going to love you and cherish you and make sure that you're okay. This has to go with one of my other tips: take care of yourself. I learned this the hard way, and the very long way. My arms were so scarred up, I didn't take care of my mental health, so I was put into emerg for two days, because I wanted to die, and I didn't talk to anybody.

So now I'm gonna leave you guys with a Dr. Seuss quote: "Be who you are and say what you feel, because those who don't mind, don't matter. And those who matter, don't mind." Thank you again, guys, so much.

Awesome! Woo!

Yeah!

This is her first twenty-minute speech, so I'm so proud of you, girl! Awesome, awesome. So, does anybody have any questions for Taylor?

They can be personal, I promise.

She's so open. (...)

I notice that you have a lot of tattoos. Which one is the most meaningful to you?

Probably one of my first which is a giraffe, and it says 'Stand Tall'. My mother designed it, and she would always tell me to keep my head above the water, and it's just always stuck with me ever since. So...

Awesome. Anybody else have any questions?

How can we help like friends and family who, like, struggle with depression and people that we know? How can we help them if we don't have any experience with it?

Do you wanna go or do you want me...?

You go ahead.

Okay. Uh, so what I find is, just be there for them. Um... I have friends who have depression as well...

I believe that Taylor's got some great messages. I love that she's willing to be so open about the self-harm, and the cutting and the anxiety. A lot of kids, what will happen is, they just go and hide it, and they're too embarrassed or ashamed to share those messages. And

one of the things that I love about Taylor is that she's really willing to open up and share those stories. I don't know too many nineteen-year-olds that are doing what she's doing. I'm so proud of her that she's not cutting herself and harming herself anymore, and she's seeing it as something that can benefit other teenagers.

My hope for them to take away would probably be that you're not alone, and that there are ways to help it. I... I hope I made that connection, um, with people. I hope that they took some stuff away from it, so...

I'm so happy for you! Finally! Cause you've been working so hard for this.

I have been.

I know. You were amazing.

Listening to Taylor speak today reminds me why I do this. It's about connecting to people. And especially young people. They're the ones who need to hear about loving themselves, and I feel honoured to give them that message.

Kelly and Rachel in the Green Room – Rachel is doing Kelly's hair before she gets on stage

 Knowing that I get to go and speak on stage at the Power in Me event with 3,000 teenagers, that is so motivating for me, because I'm gonna be able to help those 3,000 teenagers to love who they are, and to celebrate their differences.

 So we're gonna put your hair half up.

 Are we putting it up?

 Yeah, just a little.

 When I speak to teens I especially like, you know, for my ear to show, my scars showing so that they know that, you know, I'm not scared to show my scars.

 How long do you have up there?

 Ten minutes.

 Wow.

 I know. How am I supposed to do fifty years of... fifty-one years of life in ten minutes?

(laughs) Oh, you can do it.

 I've been practicing the three lessons that I'm gonna be talking about. One is about, you know, quit trying to figure out what everyone's thinking about you, and the second one is to quit comparing yourself to others, and then the third one is, um... live your passion and your truth.

 Where were you in high school when we needed that? *(laughs)*

 I know. Exactly.

 So I'm just gonna put it up right by the ear so that your ears are exposed. Do you have your elastic? Oh, there it is.

 This one?

 So there's all these teens here listening to your story about being beautiful.

 Right.

 It's going to be such an inspiration for them, hey?

 Yeah. Well, you know, it's... It's something I wish that I would have been able to have when I was a teenager.

 Right?

 Because, you know, when you're a teen, you just think you're the only one that's going through all these situations.

 Oh, it's going to be so inspiring.

Did you ever think in high school that this is what we'd be doing?

 No, not at all.

 Thirty some years later. *(laughs)*

 Yeah. It's only been twenty.

 Twenty? You liar. *(laughs)*

 Okay, hon.

 Okay.

 Are you ready? Do you love it?
{Kelly looks in mirror to see her hair}

 Oh, my god. You made me all fancy. You crazy woman. *(laughs)*

 No, it's just casual. Okay, best of luck, my friend.

 Okay. Thanks.

Kelly speaking to 3000 teenagers at Power in Me event in Edmonton

 We are so focused on being ashamed of who we are, and what we look like, and being different from somebody. And I wanna be able to get these teenagers to embrace their differences. But of course, it's hard when you're gonna open up those old wounds. And even my mom and I, we had this discussion last night, and she even said to me, "Kelly, I don't know how you do it." She said, "I would've given up a long time ago."

It is a lot of work. But I was one of those disadvantaged children who didn't know anybody that was like me. And so that's why I believe that it's so important for me to give back. Because it's okay to go through something. It's okay to walk with a limp. It's okay to be missing an arm. You know? It's okay to be blind. It's okay to be someone different.

MC: Please welcome to the stage the amazing Kelly Falardeau.

And I've learned to love my life the way it is.

You see, when I got burnt as a two-year-old, I thought I would be ugly forever. You know what it's like in school. You know how I would get called all these horrible names. Well, I remember in grade five. I walked past my teacher's desk, and I saw a picture. And it was eyes, nose, and mouth, scribbles on it, and it said "Scarface". Here's the thing I wanna share with you. I know school's tough. I know you're looking in that mirror, and a lot of you are saying "Yuck. Who's gonna love that?" I used to do it all the time. I'd look in that mirror and I would say, "Nobody's gonna love this body." And I realized that I was the enemy. I was the one who was saying I was ugly. The mirror can't talk back to me. Just like the mirror can't talk back to you. And I realized one thing. Neither of us are ugly.

(audience cheering)

That mirror does not talk. That mirror does not have emotions. That mirror does not have feelings. Those feelings are us. They're in our hearts. They're in our head. We are the ones who are in control of our thoughts and our feelings and our emotions. Every single one of you has an amazing power and energy inside of you. Every single one of you have differences. Let's celebrate those differences. Those differences are what makes us unique, special. Those differences are what make us who we are. Follow your passion and live your truth. And when you do that, I promise you, you will feel still beautiful. Thank you. I am Kelly Falardeau.

(audience cheering)

Kelly and teens backstage after the Power in Me event

 What did you guys think of today? Share with us.

 I thought it was motivational.

 You thought it was very motivational? That's awesome.

 To go through what you went through and then just come back swinging. I mean, like, it's great. It's really inspirational. Truly.

 I love the concept of the mirror and how...

 Yes.

 Everybody looks in the mirror every day and... it's not the mirror talking back to you, it's you, and it's not... the you that should be... Like, you need to tell yourself that you aren't ugly. You're beautiful and it doesn't matter what the mirror says. It's what you say.

 I need a hug. I need a hug for that. Thank you. I know. Okay, let's get in there. Come on, guys. Get in there. Come on. Get in, guys.

 Are we smiling? Is it a picture?

PRODUCER CHRIS: Look at the phone.

Kelly chatting backstage of Power in ME event

 Of course I was a little nervous. How could you not be nervous, right? It's not very often you get to speak in front of teenagers, but it was so cool that the mirror thing and, you know, make an impact that way and see the impact it had with the teens, so it was just an amazing, powerful day. Love it.

Jump for Kamp Kids Fundraising Event at Skydive Big Sky in Innisfail, Alberta

 We're gonna go up in the sky and jump out at 14,000 feet. Are you ready?

I'm ready.

 High five, let's go skydiving.

 High five. Okay, let's go.

 What I've been through, most people would describe as their worst nightmare. And because of that, I get called brave a lot. But I don't always feel that way. I get scared. But I learned that if you wanna grow, you've got to face your fears.

Kelly, Alexanna, Cody, Parker, Cam and Tandem Masters from Skydive Big Sky inside the plane

 Bye, guys! Woohoo, way to go, Parker! *(laughs)* Yeah, that's my son, Parker, my son Cody, and my cousin Cam, and my daughter Aex.

 Are you ready?

 I'm ready.

 Plane's gonna start going. Make some noise for skydiving, everybody! Woohoo!

 It would be very easy to see my life as a victim, and say, "Poor me." But I choose to see the gift in it. I choose to see that the reason I have to live through all of this stuff is so that I can teach others.

Kelly jumping out of a perfectly good plane with her tandem master (who is also a burn survivor)

 Oh, my God. Woo!

 I am who I am, so that I can teach people how to love who they are. If I can do it, they can do it, too.

The End

Kelly's Three Lessons to Feeling Beautiful

During Kelly's speech at the Power in Me event to 3000 teenagers, she talked about the mirror and how it isn't the enemy. The mirror can't talk, it doesn't have feelings or emotions. It's our thoughts we need to change to feel beautiful about ourselves.

She mentioned the three lessons.

1. Quit trying to figure out what everyone's thinking about you.
2. Quit comparing yourself to others
3. Follow your passion and live your truth.

Lesson 1 - Quit trying to figure out what everyone's thinking about you.

One of the hardest things to do is to stop being so curious about everyone's thoughts of you. We walk down the street and notice people looking at us and almost instantly we think they are thinking something negative about us. It's super crazy that we go to a negative thought so instantly! And yet, how do we know what they are thinking if they don't tell us? We don't.

People look at us for about two to three seconds and then they are back to thinking about themselves and their own lives. True story! People are way too concerned about their own lives to worry about ours. Stop trying to figure out what other people about thinking you – all you are doing is creating more drama in your life and it doesn't serve you in any way. All it does is create negative drama/stories in your head.

I used to think every time someone was staring at me, they were 'thinking' I was ugly. That is, until my friend Paul helped me to realize they might be thinking something different. He was walking me to my car late at night and we both noticed a guy walking towards us and staring at me. I said *"Ugh! Someone is staring at me again, I'm so tired of being stared at."*

Paul responded by saying *"Kel, he's staring at you because you're so darn cute!"*

When he said that, it made me realize that when I see someone who is different, I don't instantly think they are ugly, so why was I believing that everyone looking at me was thinking I was ugly? That's when I realized you can never truly know what anyone is thinking and it's crazy to make assumptions. When you notice someone looking at you, just smile at them. When you smile, it makes you look happy.

Lesson 2 - Quit Comparing Yourself to Others

Lesson number two is also challenging. It is so natural to walk into a room full of people and compare ourselves to the other women in the room. We size everyone up. Who is wearing the prettiest dress? Who has the nicest hair? Who's outfit makes them look fat? Who looks like they just had Botox? Who has the nicest shoes? Who has the worst outfit? Who's hair looks horrible? How could they wear that, they look like a slut? Who is looking old and tired?

We instantly want to compare ourselves to the people in the room and we make assumptions about how we fit in. I used to do that all the time and then I would crumble because of course, I would be the only person in the room covered in ugly scars. How could I consider myself beautiful when I was the only one covered in scars? As far as I was concerned, everyone was more beautiful than me!

My shift occurred when I learned even the most beautiful people can find at least five things wrong with themselves and most times, they don't think they're beautiful. They look in the mirror and pick on themselves just as much as anyone else. Release the need to compare yourself to other people. When you do, you will feel less stress and realize you are 'still beautiful' just the way you are; even with all your imperfections. We all have imperfect bodies and that is what makes us beautiful, special and unique. For more strategies to develop confidence and self-esteem, go to my book '*Self-Esteem Doesn't Come in a Bottle*'.

Lesson 3 - Follow Your Passion and Live Your Truth

Over the years, I have had many jobs. So many, I can't even remember them all. I used to get mad at myself because I couldn't stay at one job. I used to think about my grandma and how she stayed with one company for her whole life; 40 years she worked at the same job. I asked myself why couldn't I do that? Why didn't I have the attention span to work at the same job forever? I felt like I was unstable because I couldn't stay at one job. Why was I getting so bored and hating myself?

Simple…

Because the jobs I was doing weren't my passion. I was spending eight hours a day doing jobs I hated instead of doing what I loved. I didn't find my passion until I was 43-years-old and became a motivational speaker. That's when I realized my true passion is to inspire others. I love it; it fuels me; it empowers me and makes me feel more energy than I have ever felt in any other job. I have also been doing it for eight years now and that's the longest I have ever stayed at one job. In fact, I don't consider it a job because I love it so much. It doesn't feel like work because it empowers me instead of drains me.

The day I realized I wanted to be a speaker full-time was when my boss asked me this one question: *"Are you going to be excited to come to work on Monday or relieved if you don't have to?"*

That question hit me right to my core and I knew what the answer was. I would be relieved if I didn't have to go to work on Monday and I went into the office the next day and quit on the spot.

When my boss asked me that question; I felt like the baby bird being pushed out of the nest. I realized the baby bird never falls to the ground. She makes a little dip when she is first pushed out and then she flies high into the sky. And that was me...

I worked my butt off as hard as I could and lined up speaking gigs for myself plus launched my second book '*Self Esteem Doesn't Come in a Bottle*' plus won the Fierce Woman of the Year, YWCA Woman of Distinction and the Queen Elizabeth II Diamond Jubilee medal. I did all that in one year. So yes... it is extremely important to follow your passion and live your truth because when you do, you will love yourself in ways you didn't know you could and you will feel 'Still Beautiful'.

Over the years, I realized feeling beautiful doesn't come from what your skin looks like – it comes from so much more. It comes from how you make yourself 'feel'. You can't feel beautiful if you're calling yourself ugly names in the mirror. You can't feel beautiful if you're comparing yourself to all the other women and putting yourself down. You can't feel beautiful if you are working eight hours a day in dead end jobs you hate or if you're in a toxic relationship that is draining you and harming you.

Feeling beautiful comes from living your truth, following your passion, being in jobs and relationships you love; being with people who love and adore you, having hobbies and interests that empower you. Do whatever it takes to make yourself feel loved. Love yourself and if you don't love yourself, ask yourself why. What is it that you are doing in your life that is making you hate yourself instead of love yourself?

There are more lessons to feeling 'Still Beautiful' in the online program listed at the back of this book.

PART TWO – MY FRIENDS' STORIES

••

The rest of the book are stories from other friends of mine. Friends who I believe understand the beauty myths and how untrue they are. They understand beauty is so much more than just what you look like.

Some of my friends struggled with obesity, others struggled with addictions or sexual abuse or cancer and so much more. Each person has an amazing story that will make an impact on your life. Each person's story will help you to realize how everyone is 'Still Beautiful' even though they've struggled through a tragedy that made them feel ugly at one point or another in their life.

Author:	Story:
Trish Ellis	The Biology of Beauty
Janine Brisebois	Coffee Break
Kelly Craig	Not Fair from the Start
Dawn Lloyd	The Journey to Self-Awareness & Simplicity
Leafy Shaw-Husfeldt	Natural Beauty is Personal Strength
Liberty Forrest	The Toxic Seeds of Self-Destructive Beliefs
Loya Sales	Just 'BE' by Yourself, With Yourself as Yourself
Nicole Kraft	Transformation of Love
Sharmine Massey	The Journey of Self Love
Teresa Syms	The Exorcism of One's Own Mind & Beliefs
Vanessa Canevaro	Twists & Turns
Victoria Moon	The Gift in My Concussion
Elizabeth Macarthur	Oh No, Not My Hair
Karen Schaible	Escape from Food Guilt
Rachel Gour	How My Life's Work Made People Feel Beautiful
Madie Vilbig-King	Dear Precious One, It's Not Your Fault
Shawn McIntyre	The Journey is the Same for All of Us
Tara Oberg	The End of the Rainbow
Sylvie vanSteenoven	Cancer is Not Taking Me Out!
Kelly Wollf	Still Beautiful in a Cut-Throat World of Fashion
Ava Schriver-Dunn	I am Enough
Kimmy Ann Rose	How Could I?

The Biology of Beauty

By Trish Ellis

Have you ever wondered why some days you can feel like a beautiful goddess and on other days you feel like a troll? Well, if you're like most women, you've probably blamed it on your appearance. "I'm bloated." "My skin is horrible!" Or "I'm having a bad hair day." But those excuses aren't really why you do or don't feel beautiful. There's far more to your relationship with the mirror that you've never been told. And because you haven't, chasing beauty is a never-ending marathon.

So why is our reflection in the mirror so powerful and seductive? Why do our looks matter so much to us? Why are we so sensitive and easily inflated or deflated by our appearance and so willing to spend a fortune to feel beautiful?

The answer is complex. We give away our power to the mirror because we misinterpret what we see in it. Feeling beautiful has nothing to do with our outer appearance and everything to do with our biology. And when we understand this, we claim a life-changing superpower.

Welcome to the biology of beauty. *Pull up a chair...*

This might shock you, but what you see in the mirror isn't really you. What you see is really a filtered version of "you" created by chemical peptides conditioned into your nervous system. *Here's how your brain perceives:*

Let's say you're a 44-year-old woman with short blonde hair, fair skin, deep-set blue eyes. But that isn't how you would see yourself, is it? Your brain is wired to see things subjectively. So you'd probably see something more like this; *forever single, overweight, in-debt,* 44-year-old, with *mousey* brown hair and *pretty* blue eyes. We see things with *our* meanings and beliefs attached to them. Your brain does this for your survival. If you've been bitten by a snake, you'd naturally interpret a rope on the ground as a threat. And if you're 44 and you've never been married, you'd see yourself relative to your deeper feelings and beliefs about being single. We don't see things as *they* are; we see them as *we* are.

Our brains don't interpret things objectively. Rather, they're meaning-making machines that interpret data subjectively. They view us and the world around us through the filters of our beliefs, judgements and past experiences. Our beliefs about life, relative to the pains and pleasures of the past become the reference point of how we see and experience everything. This process takes place in the limbic brain.

You see, to experience what we call life, we need to know who we are. Your brain needs a way to communicate with your body that you are separate from one another. It creates your self-identity (a sense of separation and autonomy) through the limbic brain. The limbic brain is responsible for producing chemical peptides better known as your "feelings." Your feelings are the by-products of the thoughts you think related to your beliefs and judgments.

When we revisit specific thoughts and feelings over and over again – these chemical peptides get (conditioned) into our nervous system. We become chemical representations of what we think about the most. If we've dominantly focused mental and emotional attention revisiting past experiences where we didn't feel like we fit in, felt judged or unworthy and created stories to confirm our pains, those peptides would become our identities and our points of homeostasis. What we've focused on in the past becomes the chemical lens through which we see and experience ourselves and the world.

We think approximately 60 - 70,000 thoughts a day and 95% of them are similar to yesterday. That means our daily thoughts are grooming our nervous systems. By age 35, most of us have our identities well assumed and wired in us. And just like we get addicted to drugs, our bodies get addicted to the chemical peptides that our thoughts produce.

If self-judgmental thoughts are the dominant (peptide) pumping into your body, then your identity would likely form around insecurity and unworthiness. And here's the kicker...while no one would ever consciously choose to feel insecure or unworthy, when your body is conditioned to those peptides, it wants more. And just like a heroin addict's body goes into withdrawal if it doesn't get heroin, as you begin to think better feeling thoughts, your body is going to kick up a fuss because you're not giving it what feels familiar to it.

How the body triggers the brain...

If you've been bashing yourself for years with self-judgment, your body will become well acclimated to judgmental peptides. Your body always wants what is familiar. To get those familiar peptides it performs a ninja survival move to trigger your brain to think a judgmental thought. You'll hear an internal voice; "You look really fat in those pants." And if you take the bait and attack yourself (vs offering kindness to yourself) homeostasis wins and your brain releases more self-judgmental peptides. The cycle continues.

Your thoughts trigger your feelings and then your feelings trigger (more of the same feeling) thoughts. It's a loop. The only way to get out of the loop is to think greater than how you feel. Read that again. This means, to stop the loop; you can't buy into the self-judging voice in your head. If you do, you're stuck in unworthiness. You need to dig deep and remember what you're learning here. Your power to stop judging yourself and think more loving thoughts is easier when you understand the biological nature of the voice you are hearing. It's not the truth, it's a survival process. You survived yesterday, so yesterday's thoughts are what your body wants for dinner today.

To see your worth and beauty, you need to break your addiction to judgment. Stand up for yourself and defend yourself with thoughts that will bathe your nervous system in healthier peptides. When you begin to think kinder, more loving and compassionate thoughts about yourself and others, the lens through which you see yourself and others will change. Without the hormones of stress driving your nervous system, beauty is everywhere. You aren't ugly, unwanted or unlovable. You never were.

Few people understand this and that's why the beauty industry is a multi-billion dollar business. We get seduced by miracle face creams and lip injections because it appears our wrinkles and thin lips are the source of our problem. But they aren't.

The source of our "not good enough" perceptions lies in our nervous systems and not in our mirrors. It won't matter if you look like a supermodel; you'll see and feel your dominant emotional conditioning reflecting back at you- *unless* you're using an external high to override your emotional conditioning. *Here's an example...*

If you've just won the lottery, the euphoria of your win will temporarily override your emotional conditioning. You'll naturally feel more beautiful holding your winning lottery ticket than after you just got fired from a job. This explains why you can feel like a goddess one minute and a troll the next. The mirror doesn't show us what's on the outside; it shows us our chemical conditioning overlaid with our current emotional states.

All of us use emotional highs unknowingly and here's why they're so popular...

When we feel unattractive or emotionally low, a day of shopping, a glass of wine, or a visit to the casino lifts us *above* our emotional conditioning. It feels like our low emotions disappear with these actions, but they are only being numbed by adrenaline, a neurotransmitter. Adrenalin highs are like anesthetic. They wear off. As soon as tomorrow comes, the adrenaline high of your last purchase or new hair style begins to fade. Soon we feel the same as we did the day before. Don't believe me? Go peek in your closet. All the goodies you brought home on your high from shopping probably look really boring to you now. Right?

The beauty industry loves our lack of awareness. We empty our pockets trying to buy our beauty, not realizing that what we're seeing in our mirrors isn't our physical bodies, but rather the fullest expression of our psyches staring back at us. We are seeing the bigger picture of all the places we judged, abandoned and attacked ourselves. The mirror represents the repressed darkness where we pushed down our pains and created stories that we weren't good enough. We did this because we didn't have the emotional maturity to nurture ourselves in our pain. Instead, we believed the bullies and carried the torch for them, beating ourselves up further.

Remember all those moments you were teased, embarrassed, lonely or hurt? Your subconscious hasn't forgotten them. There's a wounded part in every one of us that lies deep in our unconscious. This is your inner child. She's begging for our love, compassion and attention. Symbolically, SHE is the person you're seeing in the mirror. But because we don't understand this, we further attack her with *more* judgment instead of offering her the love and nurturing she needs. Unaware of our missed opportunity for healing, we judge ourselves and jump back on the treadmill for the next beauty chase.

Rinse and repeat...

Back to the mall for more makeup, a booty call to an old flame, a binge on Netflix, or we sit down and eat an entire pie...all in the name of our lack of understanding. We use excuses like; "If only....I had more money. If only I was married to my dream partner or I looked like Kim Kardashian, *then* I'd be happy." But it doesn't work like that. Ask a billionaire how he feels? Ask Kim, Khloe or Kylie if they feel beautiful enough? Nope, it's not happening because the outer isn't the issue.

Our outer environments can never override the science of our inner conditioning. You can have everything you want sitting on your lap, but if your body is swimming in survival emotions like insecurity or unworthiness, you'll feel *that* and not your beauty or money. And it's nothing to be ashamed of. It's a journey we *all* walk. I believe awakening our worth is a huge part of the experience we came for. We are here to awaken to our infinite power. By understanding the power of our thoughts and our biology we are moving closer.

We are evolving beyond our survival instincts by understanding ourselves better. Chasing beauty, money and worth is painful because it's designed to be. It's the divine's way of nudging us out of the illusion of unworthiness. It's supposed to hurt when we look to our mirror, bank accounts or job title to affirm our worth. When we believe we need to be anything other than who we *are* in this moment, we will suffer.

Beauty is a soul journey, not an ego journey.

Loving the wholeness of who you are (as you are) is what will liberate you. There's nothing wrong with makeup and stylish clothes. I'm a big fan. But we need to be aware of the emotions that are driving us to them. Instead of running to the mall to avoid your feelings, sit down and FEEL them. Put your hand on your heart and talk to the little child inside you. Give her the love and compassion she needs and craves. Your relationship with her is the only permanent beauty cure. Self-love is magic serum needed to recondition your nervous system and you can start applying it today.

Take back your power from the mirror. Paste a sticky note on it: "What I am seeing in this mirror is the hurt little child inside of me. She is a reflection of all the times I didn't feel safe, loved or wanted. To see my refection change, I need to be more loving, compassionate and nurturing to her." Once I begin to offer *love* instead of judgment, my truth will begin to unfold. I won't just feel beautiful; I will feel invincibly beautiful.

*By **Trish Ellis** is The Talent Scout for your Soul. She's an intuitive coach, mentor, speaker, copy writer and creative web designer passionate about helping women awaken to and showcase their worth in their business and life. Visit www.AwakenYourWorth.com and order Trish Ellis's book 'Awakening Your Worth'.*

****

Coffee Break

By Janine Brisebois

It could have happened yesterday. I remember it that clearly, yet it was such a long time ago. Ah, yes, such a lovely summer day! The sun was bright, the skies calm and the birds twittered across the prairie farmyard. The gentle breeze washed my face with anticipation as I ran down to the well to fill our water pail. There was a sense of excitement in the air! The old yellow farm house, perched on a flat lands hill, stood ready to welcome many guests on this day – my father's birthday!

As a happy-go-lucky little girl, I loved nature because I felt safe there. All was not well at home. I had adopted a mantra. It was one said to me over and over again by a family friend and so I believed it was my truth - I was unloved, unwanted and uncared for.

May I share with you how this began? Born fifth in a family of eight, I was born Sept 15 – right during harvest! A big deal at the time. The work needed for harvest, the manual labor, the requirement of my mother to cook meals for the farm hands – all this was a huge deal. I interrupted all of that. Born in the middle of harvest, born a girl and born with a heart condition. These three things had already marked me – and I had just taken my first breath. A medical concern in a family that had little money, required to visit cardiologists in cities far from home. Mom had to arrange for someone to come out to tend to four other children. It seemed I created problems. I was even left in the hospital for a couple weeks without my parents because the medical profession believed out of sight was out of mind. They were wrong. I felt abandoned.

My mother overprotected me as I grew – meaning that she was constantly yelling at me not to run. Do you know of any child that does not run? I remember making a big decision when I was little. I was running to kick the tomcat off the queen who was wailing in what I thought was pain. I was too young to understand that it was just an act of great joy for them. Mom was yelling at me not to run. Dad was yelling at her to stop yelling at me. I decided that day, yelling was not a way to live and cats screaming would not be allowed either!

I digress.

Dad's birthday party. Relatives had traveled from far and near to be here. Not for Dad's birthday but for my parents' surprise 25th wedding anniversary held two days prior. Well, it was supposed to be a surprise – but Dad heard people talking about it on the 'party' phone line. So, even though he knew, he never told Mom. She was so surprised when she saw all the people who had come. That was a great party! It was a time of great joy!

Since the relatives lived in other cities and provinces, it was natural they would extend their stay. I thought city people were the luckiest people in the world. They lived in a city! They had so many things to do, places to shop, dressed elegantly but most importantly they had running water and flush toilets! No, we still did not have running water at our sink. We had to run to the well to pump out water for drinking and bathing. It would be many years before I understood the calming effect of the farm on the highly stimulated city life soul.

The relatives also stayed to party some more. Dad's birthday was the perfect excuse. My mother had been busy in the kitchen preparing a meal, baking the cake and visiting with her siblings. As I skipped towards the house, water pail in hand, I knew deep within me, I could put on a happy face for my relatives. Never would they know the horrible things I experienced in my short 13 years.

Like my Dad, I too could keep a secret...

Of course, I would never want anyone to know that my great uncle had molested me in that long dark hallway when I was only five-years-old. Then at age nine I was lured to come and play a game with some boys. More molestation and abuse – some game. They laughed at me as they made me do very lewd things.

For the next three years, I was at their beck and call to be molested more under the very guise that if I did not, others I loved would be hurt. Better me than them. I could not bear the thought of my younger sisters or my younger brother being abused. The final night of living in this hell was when I awakened to being raped, I was 12-years-old! In the other bed in my room were my two younger sisters. More than what was happening to me was the fear that he might do this to them. There was *no way* I would let that happen. Rather than scream out, I endured his assault quietly. I decided to become the watch guard for my siblings to protect them from this horror. I pray it worked. It was a Big Secret for this little girl to bear.

Back to the birthday party. I loved having people around. I loved to serve, and I got to serve them this day. Usually, the children would be sitting at a different table. Not today. I was 13-years-old. I was sitting with the adults. Wow, I felt so special! I had even dressed up in a pretty skirt, top and nylons!

The sun was bright, the laughter hearty and the meal delicious. Then it was time! Mom called on me to get the birthday cake. It was inside the cupboard. These tall cupboard doors built of plywood were sticky. Not because of syrup or butter or dirty hands touching them. No. They were sticky because of shifting and sometimes one had to pull hard on the door to separate the door from the frame. Not this time.

I ran quickly to the cupboard. I reached up, feeling giddy with excitement to light the candles and bring the cake to Dad. I wrapped my fingers around the doorknob. I pulled hard. Surprisingly, the door opened easily. Reaching for the cake, I saw the coffee percolator lid move. Then what seemed like slow motion, the entire percolator moved towards me. I remember thinking, "Mom is going to kill me. There won't be coffee to serve the guests."

Then the coffee hit my body, all 30 cups of freshly perked coffee and steaming hot coffee grounds. Landing on my genitals, hips and thighs. I *screamed* as I took a few steps back and faced the table. The horror of what just happened hit the faces of my relatives as they stared at me in disbelief. My aunt leaped into action, tearing the clothing off me. There I was, standing in front of my relatives, naked. Vulnerable. Shamed. Thirteen. I was rooted in place. Time stood still.

Until my Mother wrapped cold wet towels around me. The six-mile drive to the hospital was a blur. I was in shock. It was surreal. I felt no pain. When the doctor removed the towels, the air hit my skin. Pure agony. Severe burns. The blisters were already huge. The nylon threads had melted into my skin and had to be removed, one by one. The wounds were dressed and I was sent home. That was the most painful night of my life. There was no position I could lie in where I was not in pain. I cried almost all night and my Mother cried with me. We returned to the hospital in the morning. I was admitted for three weeks. Dressing changes were excruciating. This was done twice a day. Every day. I remember pulling out the nylon threads, along with the healing skin and discharge. Another event that marked my life forever.

Thanks to the special paste our African doctor concocted, the skin healed nicely - I did not. I relived that moment of nakedness many times. I believed they now knew everything that had happened to me. All my shame. The words, "unloved, unwanted, and uncared for" pulsed in my brain day after day.

It took many years for me to believe that my relatives did not see me naked every single time they looked at me. It took many more years before I told anyone about the sexual abuse and rape. The entire package of those 13 years determined my life until I decided that it did not have to be that way. Once I shared the truth of what had happened, my life began to change. I decided that no one's opinion of me would shape me. There is no beauty greater than learning that I was not only loved, wanted and cared for – but that I was also talented, lovable and special.

Only after I reached out, asked for help and told my story, did I notice my light began to radiate within me and allowed me to glow. Mother Nature is still my place of healing. Her divine warmth fills my soul and I am God's unique creation to the world. What a gift – what a blessing. I am the gift and I am the blessing. And no matter what you have gone through, you are not alone. You too are a beautiful unique gift and a blessing and YES, YOU ARE LOVED!

PS: I don't think my Father ever ate that birthday cake.

*By **Janine Brisebois BSC., RMT., M-NLP** is a successful entrepreneur and business professional with decades of personal success. Her studies in Psychology, Neurology and Communication allowed her to dedicate her life to serving people in roles as a rehabilitation counselor, educator, and registered massage therapist. She is a continuous learner who is now sharing her insights as a Motivational/Inspirational Speaker. She is devoted to empowering entrepreneurs and women shift their mindset from lack to abundance, to rediscover their dream and to act on their beliefs to achieve the life they truly want. People who work with Janine are guaranteed to ignite their inner joy. Through her workshops and coaching program, Janine will teach you to experience freedom as you create a life you love. To learn more about Janine visit: www.7DCEO.com*

Not Fair from The Start

By Kelly Craig

"There is hope beyond what you think. I believe your thoughts are just thoughts and they can be changed. I believe that each of us is connected to a higher power. You have greatness inside of you. I believe you were born with a destiny and that you can achieve your destiny and soar to new infinite possibilities." - Kelly Craig

I was born December 12, 1972, premature and underweight. Back then, you weren't allowed to leave the hospital until you were five pounds. It took a couple of weeks, but I went home to my family on December 26th, and so the journey began.

Most babies don't have memories of their time spent in their cribs. At least, I hope not. However, I have vivid memories. Being left in there all day, painting the walls with poop, and rocking my crib over to the door, calling out in hopes someone would come to get me. My sisters are 10 and 13 years older than I am. Each day, I would be there waiting for them to come home from school and lift me from my crib.

You may ask, "Where were her parents?" My dad had his own business as a pharmacist; he worked long hours and was not home much. I can't recall any memories of him from my very early childhood. As for my Mom, she was in bed; an alcoholic who didn't get up to take care of me. When I was two-years-old, my parents divorced and soon after, my Dad married my step-mother, Ann.

By the time I was six-years-old, I had to have two eye operations, glasses, and a patch. I hated having to rotate my patch from eye to eye each day. I remember crying every morning thinking everyone would make fun of me.

As a child, my experiences at home consisted mostly of big alcohol-soaked parties, sleepless nights and an absent mother. Childhood was a very independent experience. I would wake up alone, prepare for school alone, and venture out to the bus alone. After school, I would step off of the bus, venture into my mom's room, lie on the bed and become immersed in Sesame Street and Mr. Rogers until someone came home.

One night the phone rang and I answered. It was my Dad. He asked where Mom was and I informed him she wasn't home. He replied sternly, "Kelly, I'm sending a police officer to the house. I want you to let him in when he gets there and wait with him until I come to get you, okay?" I murmured a coherent "Yes" and hung up.

As the officer arrived, so did my mother and my new step-dad, Jim. They were vexed that my Dad was coming. The officer arrived and came in to check on me; I was crying and confused. I convinced him I was okay, and he left. I was peering out my mom's window for my dad. He eventually pulled into the driveway in his white Porsche. Next, I saw my step-dad walk up to the car, pick up the front of it and drop it on the ground. I watched in horror as my dad backed out of the driveway and drove away. I didn't even get to say hi to him. Tears were streaming down my face; I didn't understand why this was happening. All I could think was that I had got him in trouble and let him down. I was eight-years-old.

My senior year in high school, I used to cruise the back roads to school. I would get high before I went in. My dad had bought an old Mercedes Benz and gifted it to me when I got my license. One day I was cruising when I heard a voice say, "You're going to get in an accident. You need to wear your seatbelt." I blew it off, writing it off as a guilty conscience. On May 11th, 1990, I woke up late for school. I asked my dad to sign a note and I took my sweet time getting ready. I rolled a fat joint, got in my car, and took the back way to school.

As I was putting out the joint in my ashtray, I took my eyes off the road. I looked up and all I saw was a huge tree. *BOOM!* I slammed into a tree, dead on. I woke up in my car and tried to get out of the door but it was jammed shut. The car was still in drive. I crawled over to the passenger side and got out and started walking. I was on a back road where there were not very many houses around.

I realized I was hurting really badly and needed help. Dizziness consumed me as I fell in the middle of the road. I forced myself back up and saw a car driving towards me. The woman driver pulled over. The lady (an angel) told me to get in her car. She drove to the police station; I was in bad shape. My stomach hurt so badly and I couldn't see anything but white outlines of the trees in front of me.

The ambulance arrived. They placed me on a stretcher, and I was on my way to the hospital. I could hear them calling my dad over the radio while we were en-route. I was petrified he was going to be so disappointed in me. I totalled my car!

I remember the whole ordeal in the Emergency Room...the doctors, my dad coming in, and being told I needed surgery.

When I woke up from surgery, I found out I lacerated my liver with the impact of the steering wheel. I was in a ton of pain. I had thirty staples all the way down my stomach from the surgery. At 17-years-old, this was a huge blow! I was going to have a huge, blotchy scar down my entire stomach for the rest of my life!

And with this injury, how was I supposed to graduate in a few weeks?

After a week in the hospital recovering, I was able to go home. It was hard to go back to living after that. Even just getting in the car on the way home from the hospital made my blood run cold. I had a ton of work to make up at school, but I pressed on. I returned to school one week before graduation and spoke with all of my teachers. We worked out grades and on June 3rd, I graduated with my class, only by a miracle. This was the first time I thought God must want me here for a reason.

At 39-years-old, I found myself alone, separated, and raising two teenagers as a single mother. All my thoughts were depictions of anxiety, poverty, and hopeless despair. I knew there was more to my life than that, but I felt stuck in a rut and barely capable of surviving.

I was speaking with my oldest sister one night and I shared how I was feeling. She told me that I needed Louise Hay. I had no idea what she was talking about; "Louise who?"

She put me on hold and when she returned, she started reading from a book called, "You Can Heal Your Life." I listened intently to her talk about how a thought is just a thought and a thought can be changed. Inspired, I ordered the book after our call and read the entire thing that same night. What I discovered was the power of positivity and the law of attraction. That's when I realized the voice I'd heard at 17 was my connection with the universe!

I was fascinated as I learned how much more there was to life than just that we are on this physical plane. I started learning all I could about spirituality, angels and even the Bible. I started to pay attention to my thoughts, to how I was speaking, to how I acted, and I turned my negatives into positives. I told myself a different story, like "I am good enough, I am smart enough, and most of all I believe in myself."

Things started to change little by little. I quit smoking and joined the gym. I felt really good instead of exhausted and drained. I became unstoppable in my achievements. For once, I felt hope for my future.

I decided to go back to college. It was a promise I had made to myself way back when. I wanted to be a good role model for my kids and show them it's never too late to accomplish anything you set your mind to doing. I decided to enroll at the University of Phoenix and worked for over two years to get my Bachelors of Science degree in IT for Web Development.

It wasn't easy raising two teens, working full-time and taking classes in the evenings at home. I completed 24 classes in just two and a half years and was able to finally move out of the mail center after ten years and into the software group, where I am currently an SQA Engineer.

I left out many details of this journey I call Life but this is the main takeaway for anyone reading this: Although I was once a little girl who started life in an uphill climb from the start, I never gave up. It took me 40 years to learn that I am beautiful, smart, courageous, and worth loving. I healed "little Kelly" as I meditated and got in touch with my inner child. She was there, full of sadness just wanting to be held and told everything was going to be all right.

Each day I wake up and move forward, taking the good and the bad with grace. I know each day is a gift and I try not to forget it. When you're feeling stuck, l ask that you look around and find the beauty in all of it. The universe is here and has your back. Reach deep, find your soul's purpose and let your light shine.

My destiny is now set to share what I've learned. To inspire others, and to teach them there is more to life than what you see through your eyes. All of us have a soul destiny. If we can just quiet our minds and follow our hearts, we will soon discover our own destinies and move towards greatness. This journey hasn't been easy. I didn't just wake up one day and things were magical. I'm still here on this earth with all the drama, tragedy, and disruption but I don't see most of it.

I stay grounded and wake up each morning on purpose with a purpose. I choose not to watch the news, yet I hear what I need to hear. I am now making a difference through supporting my fellow community members and the inventors in KulaBrands. I'm broadening my horizon to reach for the stars. All of us have choices in life. I've made some bad ones and some good ones, too. We are not perfect, nor should we be. We are meant to expand and grow, each of us, in our own ways. Our world is a gift and we can open that gift every day. I'm grateful I went through my struggles and I know there will be more. It's ok though because with my inner guidance I will persevere.

The most important lesson I learned is to come from a place of service and not to focus on the material world. Now I'm able to share my lessons and help others design their destinies, to discover their true desires. My goal is to show those who struggle how to recognize their negative self-talk, their fears, and their insecurities, and go after their dreams anyway.

I hope this serves you well. I wish you hope, faith, and love on your journey to fulfilling your destiny!

Kelly Craig was born and raised in Massachusetts. She has been working for Bose since 2001, rising from mailroom clerk to Software Test Engineer over the years. Kelly is the Board Member for kulaBrands™ Community and adores all 4000 plus community members. She has a passion for Social Media Marketing, reading inspirational books on self-help, and music. Kelly is a single mother of two adult children, has three cats, and a grand-fur-baby named Chester. She enjoys helping others, making a difference through volunteering with animals, hiking, and fitness.

Connect with Kelly on Social Media or through her website: www.KellyCraigBrands.com

****

The Journey to Self-Awareness and Simplicity
by Dawn Lloyd

I have two particularly memorable days. One was the day my life changed and the second, the day I started healing.

My guess is that if you are reading this or if you have heard me speak, then you probably don't see yourself as the beauty you truly are, and I remember feeling that way myself. My wish for you is that you could see yourself through my eyes.

I was named Dawn for the very purpose that you are about to read. I am a cross between a hippy and a redneck. What that means is that I love a simpler life, but it was a long journey to this place of self-awareness and simplicity.

I lived with violence from conception until my late forties. Little did I know I had a purpose in this life, and that is to help others. Would I go through it all over again? Yes, I would because to save or change one life would be worth all the hell I have been through.

Today I am happy and full of joy. I have met the most amazing people. I have defied the odds and I invite you to do the same.

They said I would never have kids and then I gave birth to three beautiful children. They told me because of medical issues, I would be in a wheelchair by the age of thirty, but I am still rocking this life and it isn't from a wheel chair. Guns, knives, and fists threatened to end my life but as you can see, I am still here. I believe I am here to help others in finding their power and passion. So, let's turn up the music and rock this thing we call life.

I remember when the idea of being 'Still Beautiful' was a hard concept for me. I never saw myself as beautiful. Then one day I came across a mirror exercise in which I had to look into my eyes. I saw that they were passionate and as blue as they've been since the day I was born. As I gazed into those deep blue eyes, I acknowledged immense pain. That was the day my healing began and I cried for the next two days.

This is what happened and it totally changed my life. First, I had to understand that I already have all the answers within myself and they are not out in the materialistic world. It was a difficult concept for me and a lot of others, especially some people with certain religious beliefs. You are not the programming that you have had since the day you were born; you are a lot more than a set of rules.

Secondly, I learned we are all beautiful, smart, and the universe needs us to step up and discover our passions. If you're like most people and when you find yours, you might push it down or ignore it. And if you don't know what it is yet, don't worry because it will find you.

There is a miracle that goes with that passion, but if you keep looking into your past, you will struggle to see it. The past cannot be changed, but the future is in your hands. You are neither your story nor your trauma.

You are an incredible being with a gift to share with this planet.

Here is another secret. How you think others see you, is actually how you see yourself. We are all mirrors reflecting how we see ourselves, but there is something magically waiting to happen. Once you notice it, the world will change for you and it will change how others see you and you will attract amazing people into your life.

I did not learn this from a book. I had to live it, in order to teach others. I used to look at the mirror and hate what I saw. The woman looking back was ugly and unlovable and that is what I had become. Then one day, I looked into my eyes and there it was, the magic just waiting to be noticed.

I would describe you as beautiful and magical! You are loved so much, and I was created and named just for this day and time to bring you this message. I want you to ponder something; you are so special that words cannot describe the true you. What you are seeing now is not your lot in life. You are truly *destined 2 live* the life of your dreams.

First off, how do you truly want to live? Is it the dreams you dream or the dreams that others have for you? You can do what you think others want you to do, but I am here to tell you, it will not make you happy if it's not what you want. It may work for a while, but it won't last.

You are here for a reason; each one of us has a purpose to fulfill. From the time of conception till this very day, my purpose is what you are reading this very minute. It was to tell you that you were born beautiful and today you are just as beautiful as the day you entered this life. The world won't see it though, not until you see it within yourself on that day when you finally realize how truly beautiful you are.

If only you could see yourself through my eyes. All you need to do it relax and be you! The answers are here and have always been within you. Just relax and notice them. It doesn't come overnight, but that is okay because it will come, and I am here to tell you just how beautiful you truly are, and I will guide you to find all your answers within.

I just want to be clear about one thing I have learned. I don't have your answers. If anyone that tells you they do, run away from them. No one could have your answers because they are deep within you. Others can help guide you to them, but you must still discover them for yourself. You were born perfect, but somewhere along the way, corporate and worldly programming got in the way.

There are two things I want you to understand about finding your own answers. When people tell you what works for them, you could try it if it resonates with you, but do not be disheartened if it doesn't work for you. There is nothing wrong with you. It took me years to learn this lesson. I tried doing everything wholeheartedly others told me to do, but nothing worked. It simply went haywire. All the time I was beating myself up and crying, "Why doesn't it work for me? It works for everyone else!"

As it turned out, I was the one who made it complicated. The answer was simple. I am not everyone else; I am different. I have different gifts and abilities, so I had to take another approach. It turned out that the approach I had to take took less time and effort. Bingo! I am enough and perfect just the way I am.

The second thing I will teach you is such an easy lesson, but it took me years to figure it out. After living with all the abuse, beatings, guns pointed at my head and the list goes on, I was angry. I was raised in the Pentecostal Church. Every religion will tell you to forgive. I said it over and over, "I forgive," but in my heart, I could not let go. I was still angry, and I really believed something was wrong with me.

The fact is, there was nothing wrong with me. Anger and love cannot exist in the same place. I was trying to forgive in the midst of all the anger that was built up. After searching, I finally realized there was nothing wrong with me. The reason I could not forgive was because I was still in anger.

I had to go back to a time I loved my husband where things were good between us. In that space, I was able to forgive and to this day I have forgiven him in a place of love. I continued with my father and mother forgiving them in the same way. I have helped many others who were angry at their loved ones. They were hurting so deeply and once I worked with them on this process, they were able to do what they couldn't for so long. Again, you have all the answers you will ever need within yourself.

There is something I want you to understand about abusers. They do not wake up one morning and say, "Hey, I think I will abuse someone." It does not happen that way. The thing you have to understand is abusers like my parents and ex-husband were raised with programming from other abusers. People cannot teach you what they do not know. Like how I turned it around. I had a mission on this planet and I knew I had a purpose.

I also knew I had to break the cycle with my kids. When you look back at how someone was raised, it makes more sense. Hopefully, they will wake up before anyone else gets hurt. How can they teach love when they themselves have never been loved? It is passed down the generations. It is up to you to change the cycle of abuse.

I see things differently than I used to do. For example, we may see the red flags, but we tell ourselves we are not good enough and we should settle for someone we think loves us. I am a survivor of abuse and a warrior against it.

Here are some of the cold facts I have learned. First, do not bring attention to the people who need help. When their abusers think people are trying to get the abused person out of the relationship, it makes it much more dangerous for the victim. Please don't ask why they didn't leave. It is a complicated answer even they don't usually understand until they've got out and had some intensive counselling. Asking the question only makes them defensive.

I will have my book coming out later this year called "Destined 2 Dawn" and I have a plan to help all victims. It will be like a ripple effect. Don't listen to myths like, "It only happens to women." Or "She must have liked it and so she stayed."

When they say they stayed because they loved their partners, this is not the whole truth. At least a part of what they are really saying is that they are terrified to leave, whether because they have become completely dependent (often part of the abusers' tactics to keep them under control), or because they fear the repercussions in terms of their safety.

When you assume it is only men who are the abusers, good men feel defeated.

Once victims of abuse get out, gain an understanding of the dynamics of abusive relationships, and build up their lives, they will see things in a different light. I want to help others find the power and passion within and rock your life. The music is playing for you, dear; this is your dance and your ball so start dancing! I will be there, dancing along with you and I will be playing the music louder for your spirit to hear.

You might have been waiting your whole life to find the fire and joy that is locked inside you. My heart is to help you to do that. For many, the problem is, they think they have to settle for less than they truly want or deserve. If that's you, the first thing you must understand is that you are still as beautiful as the day you were born. You deserve the very best. You can do anything! Your spirit is just waiting for you to notice how beautiful you truly are, and the world will open up for you.

You are worth everything I have lived through so that I could get this message to you. The world is open to you. Turn on the music, look into the mirror and the beautiful creation you totally are and rock this thing you call Your Life! You are so worth it, my beautiful child. Remember, you already have all the answers within!

Dawn Lloyd is a Speaker, #1 International Best Selling Author, coach, results catalyst, creator of Destined 2 Dawn and co-author of Yes! I Am More Than Enough. (50 keys to rock the fear of not good enough). She uses Psych-K to facilitate a simple change that creates a powerful impact. Dawn is a power coach who inspires people to find their passion and power at the cellular level. Having lived through violence for 2 thirds of her life, she has risen up like a phoenix from the ashes and refuses to let her past define her. She believes we are here to dream and inspire the planet. Dawn loves life in its simplicity.

Yes! I Am More Than Enough. (50 keys to rock the fear of not good enough) focuses on the inherent limiting fear people have in them of not being good enough and how to help them overcome it. You are more than how you see yourself, you eliminate the fear of not being good enough and see how much you can achieve. This book takes its readers on a 50 chapter journey demonstrating steps and exercises to follow in order to rock that fear of not being good enough. You are beautiful, you just need to see it and tell yourself "Yes! I am more than good enough." Once you see this, the world would see it too. Connect with Dawn@destined2.com Facebook - destined

2 dawn.

****

Natural Beauty is Personal Strength

By Leafy Shaw-Husfeldt

I am Leafy Shaw-Husfeldt and what I want to share with you is from my heart. I hope that if you are seeking comfort or insight, you might find solace here in the words I have to share. Or perhaps you might reconnect with the natural beauty that is the personal strength that dwells deep within you, as it does inside every one of us.

Living a conscious life is very important to my well-being. Creating a meaningful life of purpose and spiritual transformation is very high on my list of personal values. I love inspiring others to see the possibilities in all things, and most of all in themselves so that they can embrace change, which is a constant in life.

It wasn't always my experience that life is meant to be playful and filled with possibilities, but this is what I have come to learn.

Throughout my life, I have been met with many challenges and hardships. This forced me to dig deep inside myself and make changes that have carved out strong characteristics in me, such as courage, compassion, humour, resiliency, faith, gratitude and so much more. I am highly intuitive by nature and although I can be outrageously loud, outgoing and bold, I am an introvert who loves quiet time for deep reflection and insight.

I have discovered that I am here to assist others in their personal journeys of self-discovery and awakening, thereby contributing to the greater good of humanity.

Sometimes, this means standing in the pain alongside someone, or providing insight and clarity in the chaos that so often smothers the breath and beauty of life. From my personal experiences, I have come to believe that what holds us back from a truly magnificent life are our perceptions, beliefs, conditions and judgements. Our history, culture and society keep us separate and have limited some of our personal potential.

I have awakened to the truth that we live on one planet. Together, we are a collective of a human species and nothing separates us from one another. We are infinite beings of nature.

Life as we know it is changing and we are awakening to a whole new way of being. Most definitely, I want to contribute to leaving a better place for the future of my girls and all children who grace this planet.

I've come to know that I am here to assist in the healing of the Collective Heart of Mothers. When every mother's heart is healed and every mother recognizes every child as her own, we will unite humanity to its fullest potential. This, indeed, would be truly beautiful.

That being said, growing up, my life didn't always reflect the desires of my heart or the person I have come to be. In my younger years, I wanted so much more out of life, but I was usually running or hiding from some painful experience, drama or trauma.

Thank God at the age of 17, after the death of a close family member one of my high school teachers introduced me to meditation and relaxation. At the time I didn't know I was suffering from traumatic grief and depression, something that would play out more than a few times in my life.

Meditation allowed me to escape the pain. I came to realize that even at the worst of times, I could find peace and beauty "in the moment" of some of the most turbulent times in life. Over the years, I have experimented with many different styles of meditation, which always resulted in my finding some peace and relief from a life filled with more than a few great heartaches.

Through all of this, I can honestly say that there were many beautiful moments of reflection and self-discovery in the process. I would certainly never have been able to say that in the midst of one of my painful, life-evolving moments or experiences. One thing is for sure, life is funny and strange and it does take some figuring out. Imagine how different it could be if we were told and educated to know that life is a series of events and processes of growth and self-discovery. That is where the beauty lies — in the rediscovering of who you really are and who you were really meant to be.

If only we were influenced at a young age to believe that we are all unique, and that our strength and beauty come from a state of health and wellbeing. To truly know we are vibrant and resilient by nature and all things are possible if we take the daily actions required to grow. We have lost touch with the sacredness of life and the daily rituals of self-care. We have forgotten how to cherish ourselves and how to take time to connect with our inner beauty. In many cases, we are starved of the basic essentials that are required. Many of us have lost touch with a sense of self-worth and self-fulfillment.

The message I would love to share here is that in spite of whatever you may be experiencing, you are, and always have been, beautiful. Just as I am still beautiful in spite of all of my pains, trials and tribulations, so are you.

Discovering my own beauty is something that I have had to learn, as I never saw it when I gazed at my reflection in the mirror. My life itself seemed painful and downright awful at times. There was the dyslexia, numerous family deaths, multiple car accidents (which left me in chronic pain), and a handful of miscarriages that added to a grieving heart and a multifaceted eating disorder that would wreak havoc whenever I had to face off with one of these life-challenging events. I was also involved in more than a few business ventures that kept me questioning what I was supposed to be doing with my life.

Growing up, I knew something was missing, but I couldn't figure out what it was. I had come to discover over the years of deep work and reflection that more than a few of us have adopted a distorted perception of ourselves in relation to the truth of who we are and always have been. The societal norm is that our beauty is found in the outward display of ourselves and our lives as a whole. This is so far from the truth - and therein lies some of the distortion we see. As a society, we are taught at a young age that beauty is measured by something on the surface of ourselves, based on our looks and appearances. That beauty allows us a pass of acceptance.

This is so far from the truth of what beauty really is. I have come to know that true beauty is something that radiates from the inside out and expresses itself in all that we do. It is a state of being and grace. Beauty is natural and comfortable and has a subtle confidence in all we do. Most of my life I felt awkward, like I never fit in. It was like I never really belonged in my body or my life. I was always wrestling with the discomfort of my own self-acceptance. I craved more than what my life had to offer. This craving filled my heart with discontent. But I understand now that it was my true beauty that kept me in a constant state of growth and self-discovery.

The benefit of this pain and discomfort was that it set me into steady motion to find something to ease the discomfort of my life. Unknowingly, I became a steady seeker, trying to uncover a cure for the ever-present ache. Being introduced to meditation at an influential age helped contribute to this calling of self-discovery.

Little did I know that the ache was my calling and that I was never alone. I've met hundreds of people who live with the same discomfort in some area of their lives - some trauma or life-changing event that affects their sense of wellbeing and natural beauty. Some people find refuge in some mind-numbing activity that becomes the coping mechanism they use to mask the pain and live with it their entire lives. Others retreat, withdrawing and settling for "what is," stunting their own natural growth and living a less-than-desirable life.

When you live from this place, you rob yourself of the natural beauty that surrounds you and is actually meant to fulfill you. I have come to know that there is so much more to life than our pain and our perceptions. If we look for it, we will find beauty in all things and in every moment. On reflection, now I realize that beauty was always there for me. It was fleeting because sometimes I looked at life through a lens that was a bit distorted due to my personal experiences and how I assessed myself, my surroundings and the world. I realized I was chasing beauty, I could see it and feel it here and there, but it was never lasting.

The great thing about this is that it kept me on the learning path. Sometimes with adverse consequences to my actions because I have to admit, sometimes I tended towards self-destructive behaviours that helped no one, least of all myself. That being said, I always grew from these experiences - sometimes with great pain, sometimes being met with great resistance. I love to call these moments "growing pains".

If you have found your way to this chapter, I would imagine that you are also seeking beauty in your life. If this is true for you, and you have come seeking to discover one nugget of information that may give you personal insight into who you are, and what you are looking for, I would love you to know, it is YOU. You are longing to know and discover yourself, and if you are searching, honour that process. Give yourself full permission to discover and create the magnificent being that you are. You, too, will then come to know your personal beauty in many ways.

You see, what I have come to know is the ache in your life is calling you to discover your inner beauty, to investigate the truths that work best for you so that you, too, may find self-fulfillment and really own your personal worth. Each of us is born whole and complete to live the best possible life. For some reason, there comes a time for many of us when we forget, misplace or even experience some traumatic event that leaves us void of the beauty that is our birthright.

Although we have come to know pain and discomfort, it doesn't mean it has to define us our whole lives. We are gifted with the truth, and truly have the ability to choose how our lives will play out. Along the way, we will find people who will challenge us and support us. When we can see the whole picture, we discover that there is balance in all things. I have met some amazing teachers along my path and I do recommend that if you find yourself in the throes of life's challenges, or you're heavy with defeat, reach beyond yourself and seek out council and guidance that will assist you on your healer's journey. You will discover the right person at the right time for the right season and reason.

When you reach out, you will start to reconnect and reclaim your bits and pieces of personal knowledge, wisdom and insight. That's when you will discover the beauty you were seeking.

Here are some solutions for reconnecting and reclaiming your natural beauty and purpose:

- Find a coach, mentor or counsellor who has successfully overcome similar challenges.
- Start a personal journal of self-discovery and self-reflection so you can begin to create an intimate relationship with yourself.

Establish a daily ritual and routine of self-care that includes:

- Cleaning up your diet with primal food essentials that are as close to their source origins as possible.
- Read books that feed and nourish your mind and change any negative thoughts and beliefs.
- Establish a daily prayer or meditation practice to start feeding and connecting with your innate spirit.
- Make time for movement in the most playful way and that engages your soul such as walking or dancing so you can connect with your body and ground yourself.
- Enroll in education programs of interest that feed your body, soul and spirit.
- Take healthy action in the areas of your life that need some attention and care.

May you come to know beauty in all you see and do ...

Much Love & Beauty,

Leafy Shaw-Husfeldt

Leafy spent most of her career in the social sector working with multiple levels of government providing coaching and counselling support services, in housing, finances, lifestyle, education and career development.

In addition to that, Leafy was born with an entrepreneurial spirit and had many business ventures along the way that usually fed her creativity and personal expression. She even won a heritage award for preserving Indigenous and Fur Trade artifacts.

Creating a meaningful life of purpose and transformation is very high in her personal values in life. Leafy believes these basics in life are at the center of everyone's well-being. She found her personal power and resilience after completing a 90-day health challenge. It had such an impact on her life it has become the foundation of her coaching services she offers at Vibrant New Life. (Check out her ad in the back of the book, special offer for the readers) www.WildNewLife.com

****

The Toxic Seeds of Self-Destructive Beliefs
By Liberty Forrest

Like many others on the planet, my upbringing was toxic and damaging. I was fed on malicious and malignant beliefs about myself, and my place in the world. They resulted in my making countless self-destructive choices as an adult, and I've spent decades cleaning up the fallout.

I don't want to blah, blah, blah about the litany of nasty things I was told on a frequent basis or the kinds of abuse and dysfunction to which I was subjected. You might well have a list of your own, in which case I'm sure you can guess, at least generally, what mine looks like.

The point isn't so much about those details. It's more about one of the single most important "Aha!" moments I've had through all my years of ongoing healing and self-discovery.

It was the day that I understood the difference between opinion and fact. It was the day that I understood that just because my mother had always said I would never amount to anything, or that I was stupid, or didn't deserve the accolades or successes I'd got, no matter how small, those were only her opinions. She crammed those and more down my throat well into my adulthood and I believed her for decades.

Until that day. Until that day I realized I let her opinions be the foundation of my belief system. And that belief system had been the foundation of my life. Those beliefs had been firmly planted deep within my soul, sinister seeds had taken root in the toxic soil of my environment.

Because of those seeds of toxic beliefs; historically, if I could do something the hard way, I did. If I could find a way to be more misunderstood than I was already; I found it. If I could make my life more difficult, when I was trying to make it easier; I did that, too. I didn't understand any of this for many years, but finally, I realized it was because those terrible beliefs had twisted their way through my soul and affected every single choice I ever made.

It was just like busting my backside to grow a beautiful garden, and then trampling the pretty little buds while planting bindweed and bramble everywhere. These plants were insane. Just this side of impossible to kill or remove. They are extremely invasive and suffocating and even the tiniest bits of roots can turn into yet another crawling, choking, intrusive plant. Their seeds were sown for me when I was very little. Toxic beliefs that climbed and hid, creeping and crawling everywhere. The bramble tearing clothing and flesh with its evil spikes. Every time I thought I got rid of it, it reappeared in a heartbeat, ignoring me completely, as if it had never been gone.

Sometimes I wasn't battling bindweed and bramble though. Just some happy little-misunderstood dandelions that looked so innocuous and pretty, a bright splash of perky yellowness here and there, trying to brighten up the garden, what could be the harm?

As pretty as they might be, they can spread so quickly and easily; they can overtake your garden and choke out your lawn in the blink of an eye.

Yeah, I know, they have some good uses, but I'm talking about having them turn up where you don't want them, just like a whole passel of uninvited relatives appearing on your doorstep, steamer trunks in hand and askin' if they can "set a spell."

There they are, all tired and sagging, a red-faced Aunt Marjory and toothless Uncle Herbert, with scrawny cousin Alma and her dim-witted husband, Melvin with their nine dirty, scruffy little offspring who are fighting and shoving each other on your front lawn.

"We ain't got no place ta sleep!" cries Uncle Herbert. "We done bin kicked outta the trailer fer not payin' the rent but it ain't mah fault that the bootleggin' moonshine market ain't great and I cain't make no money!"

You might not mind them in their trailer, and you might even enjoy a little blast of Uncle Herbert's moonshine now and then (although it'll peel the bark off yer innards). But having them there on your front lawn and in your home -- well, that's just a little too close for comfort.

As a child, I was the seed of a rose bush, buried in a garden full of invasive and suffocating bindweed with its beautiful, deceptive flowers fooling the untrained observer, as did the delicious bramble fruit.

As an adult, I saw the bindweed and bramble for what they were and spent decades trying to get rid of them, and all the other weeds that were springing up and doing their level best to destroy the garden I was working so hard to create.

For every lovely plant I managed to nurture until it began to bloom, there were several unwanted and toxic weeds trying to destroy the peaceful, tranquil, beautiful garden for which I yearned.

Still, I kept planting many different flowers and herbs, with countless colours, shapes, sizes, and textures, while learning more about the bindweed and bramble, how to dig up their roots and destroy any remaining bit of them that lurked in the soil of my developing garden.

Dandelions and numerous other weeds kept springing up - and they are still springing up here and there. I suppose they always will because Life is just like that. But my previously very shriveled brown thumb has gradually become greener over the years as I've become better at guarding and nurturing the plants I want and removing or preventing the growth of the ones that ruin my garden.

No doubt you can relate to much of what I'm saying. No doubt you have been hoeing and digging, planting and nurturing, doing your best to create a beautiful garden of loveliness in your life, while doing battle with the bindweed, the bramble, the thistles and thorns - and the Aunt Marjorys and Uncle Herberts of your life, the stuff that comes up disguised as relatively harmless but it still ruins your garden.

But if you keep focusing on what you want to create, if you keep a clear vision of that vast array of herbs and flowers, the colours and textures, that lovely, thriving garden that is how you want your life to be, you'll get better at making it happen.

And if you keep studying about how to deal with the bindweed, the bramble, the thistles, and thorns and keep learning about the conditions in which they thrive - or they don't - then you will get better at keeping them out of your pretty garden.

It doesn't happen overnight. Even the best gardeners weren't born with the knowledge they possess. Some may have more of a knack for it than others, but they still had to learn, although it may have been fairly quick and simple, at least as compared with us brown-thumbers.

And for those of us with the very brownest of thumbs, who just seemed to create one major disaster after another throughout our lives, despite our best intentions and efforts, it's just taken us a little (or a lot) longer to learn how to create the right environment in which our beautiful gardens can grow and to figure out how to make the bindweed go away - and stay away.

Better late than never; plant yourself in your garden on a regular basis, take a look around at the gorgeous plants you've helped to grow and thrive. Poke around between them and under their leaves, and look for the weeds, whatever you don't want and get rid of it.

Whatever that means to you - whatever is cluttering up your garden and spoiling the view, whatever you don't want, get rid of it. And although you'll probably have some bits of bindweed that keep springing up here and there, at least you can be aware of it and do your best to keep it from destroying the rest of your garden.

Chances are that negative, self-destructive beliefs are cluttering up your garden more than anything. And it's likely they originated with the opinions of others and have no basis whatsoever. They could be causing you to stay in unhealthy or abusive relationships. They might be the reason you don't try for that promotion or great career, or why you refuse to believe you deserve to make your dreams come true.

When you can look at the toxic beliefs that are restricting your life and understand they are not facts; you can begin to let them go and replace them with truthful statements about how magnificent you really are.

Liberty Forrest is an award-winning author and Huffington Post contributor who has written several books on inspirational self-help topics. She also writes paranormal thriller saga fiction.

In childhood, Liberty discovered her abilities as a psychic and medium. These abilities continued to develop over the years, ultimately leading her to do readings professionally. For five years, she appeared approximately monthly on BBC Radio doing psychic phone-ins for listeners. Eventually, she took to the stage, where she connected audience members with loved ones in spirit.

Currently, she enjoys working with people all over the world, offering compassionate heart-centered guidance to help her clients get unstuck and moving forward in life. For more information: www.LibertyForrest.com

****

Just 'BE' by Yourself, With Yourself, As Yourself
by Loya Sales

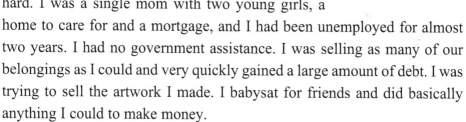

There was a time when life was exceptionally hard. I was a single mom with two young girls, a home to care for and a mortgage, and I had been unemployed for almost two years. I had no government assistance. I was selling as many of our belongings as I could and very quickly gained a large amount of debt. I was trying to sell the artwork I made. I babysat for friends and did basically anything I could to make money.

My ex is an addict who made life hard. I could never rely on him to help meet the kids' needs. Life was hard and I was stressed.

I felt horrible inside. I had a horrible attitude and saw the world the same way. The world was ugly and painful and to me, that's all life was. On a particularly hard day, I had to step back and notice what I was doing. I saw that I was acting out how I was feeling, and it made me see myself as ugly. It had nothing to do with my clothes or hair. It had nothing to do with self-esteem; it was just about my attitude. Words can be damaging, hurtful and exposing and I was not kind with my words — not to myself or others.

On that day, I was barely holding myself together. I was crying and went to wash my face. As I looked up, I didn't know who I was. I did not recognize myself through the pain, the hate and helplessness that was pouring out of me. I couldn't even look at myself as I didn't like what I saw. The lustre in my life had been fading with the trials and issues I was facing. I was not who I used to be, nor was I the person I wanted to be.

In that moment, I certainly didn't want to be me. The woman looking back at me was desperate and hurting and alone with no answers and no hope. It seemed no matter what I tried to do, everything was another dead-end road.

The pain of enduring hard times with no direction created a barricading mold over top of what I wanted and was trying to do. It made life more difficult and the pain just became something else to deal with, another burden with no end.

One night, when I was going through this dark period, I was lying in bed and I heard the words, "You don't have to hurt yourself anymore."

My first thought was, "I'm not." But to be honest, I was. What's worse is that I was doing it over and over and over again.

During the following weeks, the words, "You don't have to hurt yourself anymore," sprang into my mind quite often. They were there when I ate poorly, when I wasn't sleeping enough, or if I was using negative or defeating self-talk. The words made me see a bigger, more internal picture.

During a particularly emotionally challenging week, I made the conscious decision to ignore what was good for me. And as I did so, life became even more difficult.

It was then that I was able to see how I needed to fight the self-destructive part of myself. I saw that little steps should be big triumphs. It can be hard to work with ourselves to stay on the right path, as the longer we have been on the wrong one, the more it takes to get turned back in a positive direction.

Think of it as taking a wrong turn. The farther down that road you go, the farther back you have to travel to get back to the right road. This concept holds true for everything, weight gain or unhealthy loss, bad attitude, debt, gaming, social media, negative thoughts, use of addictive substances, anything that is self-destructive.

For example, it hurts to drink too much. People pay money for it, they get sick from it, and it alters their thoughts and personalities. Then as they continue to engage in drinking, the tolerance for alcohol gets stronger so they can drink more. That alcohol starts to destroy the liver. It creates ulcers. Internal organs stop operating properly. They have more negative thought processes, because let's remember, people destroy themselves as a way to cope with what is haunting them. Or rather, as a result of it.

Once on this path, people reach the point that what felt good as a temporary escape is now a dungeon. The body will become dependent upon it to feel better as it's being destroyed. See the cycle? 'I'll feel better while I destroy myself.'

Let's look at how having Obsessive Compulsive Disorder (OCD) can hold you back as well. There is the strong pushing force with OCD to correct what a person sees as not good enough, or not right, or dangerous. It is an irrational way of dealing with anxiety, as sufferers distract themselves with obsessive thoughts that lead to compulsive behaviours. The anxiety is temporarily relieved but as the real reason for it has not been addressed, the anxiety builds again, the obsessive thoughts take over and you're back on the merry-go-round.

For example, people with OCD might check their locks ten times before leaving home to ensure safety, as the fear of 'what if' is too great to control. If you check it nine times and a friend pushes you along, the mounting anxiety inside you becomes intolerable. You cannot enjoy your time together, you cannot relax or focus on what it is in front of you. Your thoughts take you away to a sense of paranoia.

At a point in all of this, we engage in negative talk in our heads, even when we are complaining to ourselves about someone else, or a scenario, and we say things like "I hate you," I hate life," "When are you going to do this right?" "You are so miserable all of the time, low life, get a job!"

Have you ever noticed the only one you are talking to is yourself, the only voice you hear is yours, and the only one actively listening and emotionally engaging in the rant - is you? Even if it is about your ex, or the person who stole your belongings, the only person you are interacting with is you. This type of talk is damaging to you. How can you expect to feel good about yourself?

By letting ourselves entertain these harmful actions, we are making it harder on ourselves to get back to good. As much as I want to say it's not in our nature to hurt ourselves, sometimes we do it as an escape. We can feel like someone who doesn't care, someone who doesn't need to care, someone who is in control, who has a different life, or a different perspective.

One day I was agitated. I decided I needed to change the way I felt. The best way for me to do that is to be giving. So I asked, "Okay, God, who needs some flowers from me today?" I had heard the name and even saw the spelling of the name in my mind so I knew exactly who would be getting the flowers.

When I give, I like to do so anonymously if possible. I was happy to learn the woman for whom I bought flowers for was not home when I dropped them off. Immediately, I felt a complete turn-around in my attitude and self-destructive thoughts. I felt so warm inside with anticipation of her surprise. Normally I do leave a card, and on that day I wrote, "Because you are you, and you are beautiful."

I noticed that leaving a surprise seems to create a sense of uneasiness of the unknown. So when my friend was doubting the gift was hers, I let her know they were indeed for her. She shared she was grateful and the flowers were such a blessing with perfect timing. She and her husband had been going through an adoption process. It had been a trying time and they were getting run down with the process. She saw the flowers as a sign that everything would be okay.

To be able to see and feel how much they meant to her in that moment completely cleared away all of my own anguish. I felt good. I felt good about myself and about life. I felt like I could handle things and they were a little easier.

It is renewing for me to give without expectation. It is humbling in a way I never expected. Another friend was not doing well and when I sold my camper, I gifted them generously. I didn't give them money, but I paid for an opportunity that meant even more to them.

There is beauty in compassion, in being humble and raw and vulnerable. The ability to just be ourselves, to stop and give of ourselves in the rawest form gives strength to handle the ups and downs of life.

There is beauty in stillness. In the ability to 'just be' and observe. It's not about being in touch with yourself, or with nature or with awareness, it's just being present within yourself, in the moment. It is not about wondering what you feel in that moment or what you need or what you should do. It is to just 'be' by yourself, with yourself, as yourself, with all the guards down, all the facades put away, all the different 'hats' in life taken off.

It's about not being a mom, a dad, a wife, husband, son, or employee. It is about just breathing, nothing more, and nothing less. No label attached to you, no expectation. In that moment of stillness, you are who you are: vibrant, alive, vulnerable, at peace, a soul.

Loya Sales is a strong advocate for healing one's body, mind, emotions and soul from past trauma & abuse. Her experiences make her a great candidate for the "Been there, Survived that" voice. As an abuse survivor herself, she had to identify and overcome many diversions in her life. On her path of healing, she was lead to explore and practice spirituality, as she felt the the need to find a much deeper, self connection.

In this journey, she has re-discovered her gifts and passions. Today Loya has enhanced in a stronger, innate learning and understanding of how to use what she was blessed with, to aid others in their healing journey. She loves being able to connect with others to help them see life in a new way. it is her goal to help push change. Change through healing, change in attitude, change in outlook, change in the way we process our lives. Loya can respectfully say her faith of healing has kept her strong on this painful, surprising and glorious journey.
www.LoyaSales.com

Transformation of Love

By Nicole Kraft

With Love we can change the world. But first we must love ourselves! Many years ago I started on a journey to embrace myself and who I am, where I am! All my beautiful flaws and the essential essence of myself. So many people asked me for advice and to help them, that I decided to go where the universe was leading and live a heart filled life helping others.

My journey so far has been one of tremendous growth and a testament to the strength we are given when faced with adversity. I was raised by a loving family in the country in northern Alberta experiencing what most kids did on the farm.

The oldest of three girls I got to learn a lot about perseverance and getting the job done. Early on, I knew my path was a bit different, my mom was bi-polar and struggled with severe lows, where she would be mute and catatonic, to highs of the funniest and happiest person.

Along with other life events, I was shaped and molded into the person I am. I left home at 17 to go to college to work with troubled teens journeying with others experiencing abuse and neglect, to the grief of suicide, disabilities, challenging behavior and the stories of hope.

Lucky for me, I learned skills that would help me navigate and advocate for our adoptive sons who were diagnosed with prenatal exposure to alcohol, Tourette syndrome and anxiety. Our boys came to us from my cousin, herself a beautiful soul, who faced addiction, homelessness and eventually died of AIDS. She left a legacy of love and caring and I try to pass that on.

I seek to help others see the goodness they have inside them. Showing that you can love yourself even if you feel uncomfortable within your body and living with our naked truths. We all deserve to live a joy filled life. I myself was diagnosed with Idiopathic Intracranial Hypertension, which is extra spinal fluid on the brain. For others this disease has led to blindness and tumors, luckily I only have slight vision and hearing loss. These events have made me rethink my purpose in life and tune into my passion of storytelling and helping others tell heart stories with honesty and humor.

With over 25 years working with people I have learned relationships and connections are what love and life are all about. I have travelled to India, Mexico, the Caribbean and throughout North America sharing my message and always being asked:

"Where do you get your confidence?"

"How can I find that within myself?"

Really, we all want to be happy and well, to be supported and healthy despite living with a disability, illness, addiction or mental illness. It's how we manage it. It's simply focusing on our positives and building on them, internally rewarding ourselves and making life and living fun again.

Nicole Kraft is a mother of two wonderful boys and currently resides in northern Alberta. She has been lucky to work with youth and adults with dual diagnosis of mental health and developmental disabilities throughout her 25-year career in social services. This has come in handy helping her navigate and advocate for her adopted boys and other family members who themselves have had struggles with mental health including anxiety, bi-polar disorder, Tourette's syndrome, OCD and PTSD.

Nicole has overcome living with idiopathic intercranial hypertension, which is extra spinal fluid on the brain, depression, infertility and learning herself and her naked truths. A free spirit and relationship facilitator Nicole seeks to meet other souls along their journey and collaborate to increase joyful living and happiness.

****

The Journey of Self-Love

By Shar Massey

The terms 'beautiful', 'gorgeous', and 'pretty' were so foreign to me when I was a teenager. I craved to hear these words, but I knew I was asking for too much because the mirror only showed me someone who didn't have the most desirable looks. I was chubby, had a dark skin tone, a boy haircut (really short) and was not at all attractive. I always wondered, how come my family looks so amazing; my parents are both good looking, my sister is gorgeous and my brother is handsome? I was convinced I was adopted because I didn't resemble my family at all. As a result, I had very low self-esteem and low confidence.

Teenage girls do not wear make-up was the rule in our house. My sister and I were told, girls your age have natural beauty, so embrace it. Natural beauty sure sounds good, but I didn't see it when I looked at myself in the mirror. Back home (Pakistan), being light-skinned, skinny and having long hair were apparently what make women look beautiful and appealing. My sister sure met those standards; and as a result, her confidence level was very high. I wasn't jealous of my sister, but I sure admired how she carried herself without any make-up. I always got compared with my sister either for her looks or her intellect. One cousin did not hesitate in telling me, "Your sister looks better than you" and a name I got called constantly was 'Blacky'. The sad part was that it wasn't outsiders who were putting me down; it was my own family.

School was no different. I was surrounded by beautiful girls and got bullied there too, for my looks. I started to close myself off from everyone. I was really shy. I didn't make any friends because I figured no one would want to be friends with an ugly girl. This was also partly the reason why I wasn't doing well in school. I felt like such a loser. The frustrating part was I didn't know how to take care of myself so finally, I decided to accept and compromise with that life.

Later on I started to notice boys didn't have to meet the society standard of being 'beautiful'. So to hide my lack of confidence, I started to dress and act like a boy; black jeans and boy t-shirts were my favorite. As I masked the reality and started living in an illusion, I started to believe it. At one point, I was convinced that God made a mistake when he created me; I should have been a boy and not a girl. I remember going up to my parents and telling them, "I am your son, not your daughter." I think my parents just thought I was being silly and didn't think it was a big deal. But, now that I think about it, it *was* a big deal. Psychologically I was a mess. How could I not be? I was always so lonely, depressed and insecure.

In 2000, my family and I moved to Canada. I started going to high school and continuing my education. Nothing about me had changed; I was still the same old low-confidence gal, feeling unworthy and unwanted. However, things started to change. My fellow students would actually communicate with me and invite me to join their group of friends. 'That is strange,' I thought to myself. 'I am not used to being talked to without being bullied.' It sure felt good, but I was hesitant to hang out with anyone, even though these girls were genuinely making an attempt to get to know me.

It bothered me I wasn't able to accept this amazing offer of friendship from other people. I questioned it and figured they were just feeling sorry for me for sitting alone. I also feared that once I hung out with them, they might make fun of me. I was so beaten down by all the bullying over the years that I was in disbelief someone would actually want to be my friend.

I started to read people's body language, their tone of voice and their gestures. The more I analyzed, the more I learned I am in a different environment... an environment where looks are not everything... I felt safe. There was no questioning my fellow mate's intentions but I certainly questioned myself a lot. The problem was with me.

With years of being beaten down for my looks, I closed myself off so much I wasn't allowing anyone to come into my space due to fear of being bullied again. I realized, until I love the person I see in the mirror, it would be difficult and challenging to accept love and acceptance from others. For the first time, I felt I was in a safe environment. Just months in a new country and school and not even once did I get bullied. That in itself was an indication for me that I could be loved and accepted for who I am, provided I allow that to happen. It had to start with me.

In order to accept myself and overcome my fears, I first had to love myself. I had to allow myself to feel worthy and deserving of the blessings the universe had given me. I had to let go of all the negative and hurtful feelings I was still carrying with me and allow positivity to come into my life. I decided to get out of my comfort zone and make new friends. I could be myself around these people and that was the best feeling. I could feel confidence starting to kick in. The girls around me inspired me to take care of myself so I started learning how to dress up, how to do my make-up and how to carry myself with confidence.

Then one day in school, one guy called me beautiful. That actually shocked me for a bit. At first, I didn't think the comment was for me, so I started looking around to see whom he was complimenting; surprisingly, no one else was around me. Then I looked at him and confirmed, "Are you talking to me?" He chuckled and said, "Yes. I am talking to you, you are beautiful." This is the very compliment I always craved. I never thought I'd live to see the day where I would receive such a lovely compliment. It felt so good; I had a rush of positive energy.

Things changed for me when I started to love myself… unconditionally. I struggled with the insecurities about my looks for a very long time, but then learned to see the beauty in myself and the tables were turned. You cannot control how others see you or what assumptions they make about you or your appearance, but you can certainly control your reaction to those assumptions. Being confident in yourself and your body will help you to set the standard of how others should treat you. Confidence will help you overcome any fears or uncertainty you may have and it's also a way to communicate to others that you are a powerful and a strong woman and you deserve nothing but the best.

Self-love is not a term we are taught; however, it is definitely a term we should apply in our day-to-day lives in order to be happy and fulfilled. It's good to strive to do your best and to work on being the best version of yourself but don't be too hard on yourself because no one is perfect in this world. So, love yourself with your imperfections and flaws and take pride in yourself and you will glow with confidence.

The next time you are looking at yourself in the mirror, take the time to admire yourself... your eyes, lips, hair, smile, body etc. Even when I wasn't feeling too great about myself, the one thing I loved about myself was my eyes. I saw that they were an attractive quality about me and it made me feel like the most beautiful woman.

We are often our own worse critics and it also doesn't help when we compare ourselves with others. Remember, you are a unique individual and no one else is like you. When you compare yourself, you are only disrespecting yourself. Hence it is important to self-reflect. We all have an illusion to look a certain way and when the mirror doesn't show us that, we tend to hate what we see. That's the very moment where you need to take control of the negative thoughts and allow positive thoughts and words to flow. Look at yourself in the mirror and say to yourself, "I love myself! So what if I am not how society wants me to be? I am unique in my own way. I am amazing. I am beautiful!" Those are powerful words and when you say them to yourself, you will feel a lot more confident and empowered. As a result, others around you will feel those confident vibes from you too.

And most importantly, *keep smiling!* This is the sexiest curve on a woman's body.

So... are you ready to see yourself from the lens of self-love and self-appreciation? Are you ready to compliment yourself and become the confident, empowered woman you were born to be? Then let's begin this journey of self-love.

Sharmine Massey (Shar) *is a life coach, an author and a motivational speaker. Self-love is what she practices and loves talking about. She delivers a powerful message that drives home the value of loving and respecting yourself. Shar has her own YouTube channel called "Chit Chat with Shar" where she uploads her motivational videos. She is passionate about building relationships and coaching people to make the choices that create an effective, balanced and a fulfilling life.*

Shar recently published her first personal development book called "Truly Living? or Just Surviving?" This book is focused on the importance of self-love, embracing our imperfections and overcoming obstacles in order to transform our lives. This book will influence you to reignite a positive relationship with yourself simply by loving yourself unconditionally. Shar hit her biggest rock bottom when she battled a failed marriage. That experience took her down for a little bit; however, when she came back up, she was stronger and wiser than ever before. Her life reflects on the choices she made to rise above all her circumstances to being a fearless, powerful, and a confident woman she is today.

https://www.youtube.com/results?search_query=sharmine+massey

****

The Exorcism of One's Own Mind and Beliefs

By Teresa Syms

A tiny, crippled baby girl was born on June 7, 1960. Unloved and unwanted by her mother, brutalized and sexually assaulted by her father, she was allowed to be the main source of torment for her older sister. This little girl was born with an enormous burden to carry. Her name is Teresa.

Her deformed legs were straightened at birth and for the next two years she was in full leg casts with a steel bar between her feet. What this baby needed was love, compassion, kindness and nurturing from her family. What she got was a detached, emotionally unstable mother who cared little for her; an alcoholic father who brutally beat her, and a sister who hated her very existence.

As Teresa grew, the beatings and psychological torture from her family intensified. The girls were left alone before and after school. Under the care of her sister, Teresa was never allowed in the kitchen to eat breakfast or make lunch for school. From the tender age of five, she existed on one meal per day, thus giving life to an eating disorder.

If she misbehaved at meal times, her one meal per day was denied as punishment. Being physically removed from the table, Teresa was forced to kneel in front of a full-length mirror on beer bottle caps her father had nailed to plywood (pointed side up). As she knelt, the spikes of the beer caps dug into her knees. Her sister would flash a sadistic, cruel smile and whisper, *'You're FAT and UGLY'*. The psychological damage was taking root in the little girl's core beliefs.

'You're FAT and UGLY', was voiced often. The teasing, torment and torture continued for years, but at the same time, Teresa was growing tall, athletic, and strong and was quite attractive. She had long, sandy-blonde straight hair, large dark brown eyes and a smile that lit up the room, (when she smiled). Teresa was complete opposite to her sister. Her looks attracted a great deal of attention from men of all ages. Finding the unwanted attention an invasion to her soul, she grew to believe she was, *'FAT and UGLY'*. So why would they approach her so often?

At fourteen, Teresa fell in love with a young man who was kind, gentle and quiet. They became inseparable, and her confidence grew. He was her rock and filled a void in her life. He loved her and gave her a sense of security and peace she had never known. However, as relationships go, theirs became rocky and he began comparing Teresa with other girls he found attractive.

"Your hair isn't long or blonde enough." "She is shorter and thinner and looks hot and sexy in a bikini," he would comment.

With each cutting word, Teresa's confidence decreased and depression grew. When their relationship ended, she found herself isolated and again subjected to her sister's heartless and cruel criticisms. Teresa believed she was, *'FAT and UGLY,'* unwanted and unlovable.

To ease her pain, Teresa turned to alcohol at fifteen-years-old. When alcohol alone no longer numbed her pain, she began mixing it with the tranquilizers her mother insisted the doctor prescribed. Her mother believed that medicating her would snap her out of her depression.

During this time, the constant attention from men continued. Still believing she was *'Fat and Ugly'*, Teresa couldn't understand why they approached her. When she was partying, drunk and trying to create an escape, she was vulnerable. In her loneliness, she soon gave in to the male attention. There was always someone who *wanted* her, and in time she understood their motive. They wanted sex.

Having been sexually assaulted by her father at ten-years-old and by her family doctor repeatedly in her early teens, Teresa assumed giving in to sex was how to make someone love her. She knew it was wrong, but the desperate need to feel wanted was a powerful drug for her self-destruction.

During her teen years, Teresa existed on very little food, lots of alcohol, and prescribed medication. Her mind was a battlefield for loneliness and confusion. Every day her self-loathing increased while her family life remained a ticking time-bomb.

Despite burying herself in many sports, her main love was bicycle racing on an indoor velodrome. Teresa could never outrun the painful words the plagued her mind. Always having a larger build than most girls, she was strong and well-muscled. The summers of endless back-breaking tobacco work added strength. But it didn't matter how fit she was; she always saw herself as *'Fat and Ugly'*. She saw every flaw, every ounce of fat, and every mark was another battle scar. She saw and lived what had become ingrained in her mind.

By seventeen, Teresa had developed an untouchable loathing for herself. Her sister's words had wormed their way into her very existence. She rarely looked in a mirror and when she did, all she saw was an abused, fat and ugly girl looking back at her. She also saw a borderline alcoholic, who was depressed and used sexual encounters to escape the loneliness, isolation and psychological abuse of her home life. Mostly, what she saw was weakness.

Teresa believed only a weak person would allow the violence and verbal battering she received daily. A weak individual needs medication and alcohol to survive. A weak person would accept such destructive, hurtful words. Where was her strength, her fighting spirit, and her truth? She had fallen too far down into the black pit of self-destruction.

Self-esteem, self-compassion, self-love and self-awareness were foreign to her. Teresa believed what she heard. No longer caring about herself by nineteen, her life hit critical stages. Unable to find comfort in the many relationships she had, one night she decided she'd had enough. Suicide was the answer.

The next afternoon, Teresa began drinking heavily. Never being hungry, she skipped dinner and went to her room. Listening to music usually gave her comfort, but this day, she found it fed her downward spiral. The hate she felt for herself pulled her into the bottle of pills. Nothing changed. That evening, Teresa got behind the wheel of her father's car. Her destination was a massive old maple tree in the country. She had memorized the location because she raced her bicycle past this tree often and knew it was her destiny. The pain in her heart was unbearable and she knew there was no fight left to save herself. Life had been beaten out of her.

Tears streamed down her face as she made her last turn towards her death. Sobbing uncontrollably at the injustices of her life, Teresa turned the wheels to the right for final impact. As the wheels crunched on the gravel, a peace washed over her body. She no longer felt the effects of the pills or alcohol. She was sober and very aware of her decision.

Seconds before impact, the steering wheel was wrenched sharply to the left, pulling the car back on the road. As the vehicle slowed, as voice whispered to Teresa, *"You're not finished here yet."*

In shock and disbelief, she turned on the interior lights expecting to see someone with her. She was alone and crying out a lifetime worth of pain. Teresa felt comfort and encouragement. Later, as she lay in her bed, Teresa knew she had just received a miracle.

Soon her sister was no longer part of her life, having become pregnant at seventeen and then married off. Even though there was no contact, she still heard the words, 'Fat and Ugly'. She heard them in her own head, she heard them attached to every good comment she received, always believing people were lying to her.

In time, Teresa met and moved in with a young man she believed was her soul-mate. Believing this was love, Teresa gave everything she had to this relationship. The beginning was good, until he embarrassed her by passing out drunk at a party. She verbally chastised him but was unprepared for his reaction. His response destroyed her world.

The back of his hand smashed across Teresa's nose causing a loud crunching noise and temporarily blinding her. Stopping the car in the middle of the road, she grabbed her face expecting to find blood. When her sight returned, she noticed he was asleep in the passenger seat. Silently sobbing, she drove home, then left him asleep in the car and walked into the house.

Later, he came crashing into the house to confront her, and she stood her ground. While this 6'6" angry man cursed at her, it was when his fist came flying at her face, she moved quickly, which caused him to break his hand on making contact with the door. Hours later, he begged her to drive him to the hospital.

Believing she had nowhere to go, Teresa stayed and ten days later, with his hand in a cast, they were married. After twenty-five years together and having her nose broke two more times, Teresa woke up to the fact her marriage was a battle ground of insanity. The man she thought she loved had taken the place of her sister and she was fighting back. Nothing she did was right. She was always compared to others; she spoke incorrectly, walked wrong, acted wrong, everything about her was wrong! She had lost all confidence in herself.

Later, unable to work due to a back and shoulder injury, Teresa's children became her world. She cooked, cleaned, and tried desperately to give them a home where they were loved and wanted. Unfortunately, as the years went by, her sons learned from their father how to treat her.

Now at forty-years-old, Teresa knew she had one chance. She enrolled in college to re-educate herself, while keeping her plans of her freedom to herself. Over the years her weight had increased, leaving her husband with a sense of dominance over her. He took great pleasure in criticizing her. "Look at you!" he would say. "Who would want you?" Despite his comments, her plan was set, and she would soon be free of him.

At forty-three, Teresa moved out on her own and went to college full-time. Soon she met and fell in love with a great man who worshiped and supported her. Both had been abused by their former spouses and understood triggers. They provided each other with healing love.

When Teresa turned forty-six, she graduated college and landed a great job in Human Resources. Life was incredible! Her boys visited regularly, and her live-in step sons were showing signs of growth.

In 2006, Teresa married Don. They were happy, courageous and faced every challenge together.

Eight months later, Teresa was almost killed in a head-on car accident. Seconds before the impact, as she screamed out in terror, she heard, *"You're not finished here yet."*

Severely injured, as she waited for the emergency transport, she struggled to choke back the fear in her throat. Unable to feel her legs or move her neck, she felt betrayed by life once again. She lost her job and spent the next several years in treatment for a brain injury, muscle damage throughout her body, her third severe whiplash, severe spinal damage and Post Traumatic Stress.

All the horror that was her past life flooded back and compounded her now broken body and fragile mind. "Why?" was her only question and it went unanswered for several years.

I am Teresa. Many years after my accident, I explored hypnotherapy, and past life regression therapy, and received exceptional guidance and care. I walked into my own life and true power for the first time.

I found my courage and felt stronger than I had ever been. In time, I was able to understand and come to peace with the abuse and trauma that was my past life. Continuing my journey, I wrote my first book, *'A Century of Secrets'*, in which I exposed the horrors of my life, the neglect and trauma that almost destroyed me, and the cycles of abuse, and self-destruction that have encompassed generations of my family.

My life-long passion of writing came into play as I dove deep into my second passion of helping people through their darkest times. Despite my background, I was always the go-to person when people had problems. I immersed myself into becoming a Certified Life and Assertiveness Coach, which not only helped me with residual painful issues, but provided me clarity and a solid understanding of the words, *"You're not finished here yet."*

By working with my hypnotherapist and creating a 'safe' place in which the "little, neglected and abused Teresa" could grow up, I healed my wounds and am now armed with an understanding of human behaviour.

As a coach, I encourage my clients to stand in front of their mirrors and embrace every beautiful detail of themselves. Even their perceived flaws.

After surviving years of abuse, neglect, humiliation and depression, I have learned the art of self-compassion, self-love and finally, self-respect. I can look in a mirror and know the words, *'Fat and Ugly',* are **NOT** me. I look into the dark brown eyes and see a woman who has survived many traumatic events and is strong and beautiful. I am a woman who protected her loving, kind and compassionate heart.

As I age, I understand I can never be the athlete I once was, or the young woman who modelled bridal clothes. I have curves where I don't want them as well as greying hair and wrinkles, but all those things add up to make me who I am…

I am Still Beautiful and for the first time in my life, I believe it in my heart and soul.

Teresa Syms is a Lifeologist, Intuitive Life Coach and Award-Winning International Author. For many years, Teresa has guided friends, family and clients through the process of taking a hard, honest look deep within themselves, to cause a reawakening of their dreams that provides the necessary healing to manifest success in life.

Teresa draws from a rich knowledge and foundation from true life experience, education and certifications in Human Resources, Assertiveness, Life Coaching and NLP.

Through proven action plans designed to manifest healing, growth and success, Teresa walks her clients through their Limiting Beliefs, Fear and Doubt, and clearly demonstrates that a brilliant future is theirs to be had. She is a champion for her clients and encourages everyone to break free of the silence and fear that prevents their true growth.
www.TeresaSyms.com

****

Twists and Turns

By Vanessa Canevaro

Life is filled with a million beautiful twists and turns that eventually lead you to the perfectly imperfect human being you become. I wish I could have assured a shaky and depressed 17-year-old me that the adventure I was about to embark on would eventually shed a happy ray of hope over the memories from years of childhood bullying that were crammed into my diary.

It's crazy to think that I can pinpoint the day when I first felt inadequate. I was sitting at the back of a row of grade two desks and looking to the left to see two boys who had failed the previous year pointing at me and laughing. That was 40 years ago, and I can remember it like it happened an hour ago. Quickly, I turned to face the front of the room but couldn't stop wondering why they were laughing at me.

That was the first day of grade two and the beginning of a self-deprecating spiral that would haunt me for many, many years to come. Stepping back and looking at it now, I don't know why I tolerated the bullies or why since that day, I have always clung to the negative remarks people used to describe me, and not cherished the glowing qualities I have always had. Even now, it stirs up negative emotions, which is almost tragic because in 40 years I have accomplished so much.

I have never been thin. I hid from the bullies in elementary and middle school who had given me a broken self-image. Feelings of ugliness and unworthiness were my companions. I was constantly reminded of how worthless I was by being called fat, ugly, lard ass, stupid, pig, cow, or tank, and hearing I was hated because I was overweight.

Growing up, I was a depressed kid. I hid diet pills in my jewelry box and would try to starve myself in desperation to lose weight. When I would break down and eat something, I felt like a failure with no self-control. I was exactly what the bullies thought I was and the cycle kept playing repeatedly. Back then, nobody talked about depression or positive self-image. I was just moody or difficult. I was emotional and cried often. I planned ways to kill myself and prayed God would just let me die because I was a worthless nothing.

It was two days before my 17th birthday and fifty days since my last period. I stood in front of the mirror rationalizing how the stress of grade 11 and the on and off attention of a very unstable boyfriend was causing me anxiety and messing with my cycle. In my heart I knew I was pregnant, but my fear of having actual proof kept me spinning to alternate reasons for my lateness. I made an appointment with the first doctor who could see me that day during my lunch hour and held my breath. Three hours later I would find out I was going to become a mother. I was terrified.

I had dug myself deep into a relationship with a psychologically abusive man who constantly compared me to other girls. He would end our relationship every other weekend and he slept around. "You're perfect except for one thing," he would say. I never had to question what that one thing was; I saw it every day in the mirror.

Finally finding a boyfriend meant I wasn't totally disgusting, so I tolerated the relationship and justified why I hung on to it so desperately. Who else would want me? I was still fat, awkward and ugly.

Growing up with a baby wasn't easy. I was a teenage mom trying to write final exams for grade 12, be the parent my baby deserved and desperately mediating between parents who loved me, and a boyfriend who saw us as option #3 after his friends and drinking.

Slowly, I slipped back into my lost thoughts of hopelessness and decided to look for help. Counsellors and helplines didn't exist then in rural Saskatchewan. I was referred to a public health nurse.

I waited in a boardroom with my baby sitting beside me in his car seat. The nurse came in and smiled, "So how can I help you, Vanessa?" I told her about the push and pull. That I felt unworthy, scared, stupid and irresponsible. I was defeated and broken. "I don't know what I can do for you, I'm not a counsellor," was her answer.

It had taken everything thing I had to reach out for help and her lack of compassion was like a slap in my face. I looked down at my angel nestled in his blankets, his little pink cheek squished against the side of the car seat. He opened his eyes and for the first time started to giggle. I knew at that moment what I needed to do. It was time I had better 'adult-up' and take responsibility. I needed to give him the life he deserved.

The destructive relationship with my boyfriend continued for another two years. I graduated college while supporting a lazy boyfriend from the funding of a student loan and incredible parents, with whom my son lived with during the week and who I saw on weekends and holidays home from college.

When I moved back home, I started to 'get' what being a responsible adult meant. I worked a full-time and a part-time job and barely saw my son. The old boyfriend kept hanging on like a scab that would never quite heal. The thought of "Who else would want me?" kept playing in my mind. I was dragging my child through a life I had begun to resent.

The turning point came the day I met the man who would become my husband.

Now, I don't believe you need to have a partner to define who you are in order to discover your 'best self', but I do believe we skip over our unique qualities because it's easier to see what's wrong than what's right with ourselves. Sometimes having someone round the broken edges of our imperfect puzzle and gently fit the pieces back together while still loving the gaps that don't quite fit right is exactly what's needed. For this, my husband will forever be my greatest blessing.

For 30 years I have been on a journey to understand why I can't quite let go of the past. Why there are still days when a look or comment takes me back to the tormentors in elementary school or while trying on clothing I can hear that voice comparing me to the other girls. Why is it we tend to let the painful thoughts linger and joyous accomplishments fade so quickly? Why do we seek the approval of others to feel accepted when everything we need is already here?

In life, you have two choices: Let your circumstances have power over you or find your power from your circumstances.

For a very long time, I let my circumstances dictate the direction my life was going and that led me to a life of struggle with food, money and worthiness. The comfortable thought of, "Well it's always been this way" justified why I was overweight, why we scraped for money at the end of each month and why I couldn't appreciate compliments, success and dreaming of something more.

Twenty years ago, I read a very powerful story that opened my eyes and caused me to totally flip my thought processes from justifying my broken thinking patterns to accepting the responsibility of learning from what I lived and moving forward. If I stayed where I was, nothing was going to change and I would feel horribly out of control for the rest of my life.

The story was about a young woman in the emergency room at the hospital. The woman was barely clinging to life. Her face and body were badly damaged, and it was apparent the horrific accident she had been in would quite likely take her life.

As the young doctor started his physical assessment of the patient, he noticed the nurses weren't as shocked at her appearance as he had been and he felt very uneasy about their apparent lack of concern for this poor soul. He asked if any of the nurses knew her and was surprised at their response. This struggling woman was a frequent visitor to the ER. Her horrific injuries were not from a car accident, but from the hands of her abusive husband and they knew if she survived this episode, she would be back again.

This story had a huge impact on me. I've never been physically abused, so there is no way I can understand the feelings and reasoning for people who choose to go back to their abusers. I have been psychologically broken to the point where I wanted to end everything, and I never want to feel that helpless again. I never want to kneel at the foot of my bed digging my nails into my hands while praying for God to let me die because I couldn't bear another day at school. I don't ever want to hit my head and face with a hair brush again because I hated the ugliness looking back in the mirror, and I don't want to create an escape plan for running away to make others pay for how they caused a ten-year-old me to feel.

I wasn't willing to let my sons think the way I had thought for most of my life, and if I wanted that pattern to stop, I needed to break it. I decided to change my 'normal' into what I consciously chose it to be, not what my past was dictating it should be.

I began asking for help from the person I loved and trusted and who started breaking down the walls I believed had been built from pride. I saw them for what they really were, barriers I had created to keep the painful feelings out. But by doing that, I had also filtered out the sense of accomplishment I had needed because I thought I was unworthy of those accolades and didn't deserve them.

I started paying attention to what I was thinking and why those negative thoughts kept lingering. I began asking myself if that thought served me and my life plan, or was it pulling me back into the muck of the past. I recognized what situations triggered my thoughts. Why was I so easily lured back to feelings of inadequacy and self-loathing and why was I comfortable feeling that way? Only I could answer those questions by looking deep within myself without using my usual technique of rationalizing the choices I have made because of my past experiences.

Now, my life is totally different, and I feel a newly alive freedom I've never experienced before. Looking back to ten years ago and seeing the woman I was then and the woman I have become, a definite evolution has taken place. Ten years ago, I would never have had the courage to share the turmoil I had felt because of childhood bullying. I would never have admitted to anyone that I had hated myself so fully I was willing to die or run away to avoid the pain of another school day.

Today, I've taken myself to a whole new level of self-acceptance and belief. I use my past as a tool to help others peel back their old toxic beliefs and replace them with new affirmations. Seeing my past pains as my power has helped me not only give back to those who feel broken and deserted, but also given me a renewed hope that YES there is a whole new movement taking place with a different level of understanding.

Today I'm blessed to coach people and help them realize they are limitless and can build a life they were destined to live. Five years ago, I would never have believed I would lead a team of international business people in changing their lives. Ten years ago, I would never have believed I would successfully, profitably, publish three books and 28 years ago I would never have believed I deserved to be loved the way I am today.

Steve Maraboli said, *"There is nothing more rare, nor more beautiful, than a woman being unapologetically herself; comfortable in her perfect imperfection. To me, that is the true essence of beauty."*

To me, YOU are beautiful. Let your light shine so brightly that the world has no choice but to see it.

Vanessa Canevaro is the author of three books, a successful top income earner, sought after trainer and motivational speaker who inspires others to live their dreams. She has a background in education, was bullied throughout her childhood, and was a teenage single mother who left a psychologically abusive relationship. Vanessa's road to self love has had many detours and potholes. Now, living 'The Dream Big Life' and stepping over the past has given her the motivation to help others realize their own 'super powers'.

"We are all here to help each other along", has been her life motto and she continues to live by those words as she inspires others to rise above and find their own greatness within. Her just go-for-it attitude has energized others to pursue their passions and start living their dreams. She and her husband share a home in beautiful British Columbia, Canada and have three extraordinary adult sons.

The Dream Big Life at http://www.atrua.com/
www.TheDreamBigLife.com and www.DreamBigMentors.com

****

The Gift in My Concussion

By Victoria Moon

School can be a really tough time in your life. I know that personally, because for me it was awful. You see, I suffered from a pretty major concussion in my grade ten year (15-years-old). My horse was tied to the fence while I was grooming her, and she got spooked. She reared up, catching me on the side of my head with her jaw on the way up and again on the way down. Since then, I've had a multitude of issues that all stem from a pesky brain injury. I've had to learn the hard way, an event such as a concussion can occur in a second and it can have a major effect on your life for years to come.

Because of my concussion, I missed lots of school. I know, most teenagers would love to miss school, right? Not me.

Up until that point in my life, I loved going to school. I was the top of most of my classes, and while I didn't like math I could still hold my own and achieve 80% most of the time. School was also a great thing because I got to see my friends every day. My view on all that changed instantly after dealing with my concussion.

I didn't even know I had experienced a concussion until I went to a neurologist a short while after an incident in band class. When I was playing, suddenly I could not read my sheet music anymore because the notes appeared to be dancing across the page. That, coupled with the fact my frequent headaches had started turning into migraines, is what pushed my parents to take me to the neurologist.

He's the one who told me my brain was beaten up, only he said it in much more medically-accurate terms than that. He even gave me an unofficial list of do's and don'ts, which didn't thrill me too much. Don't go on screens, don't do anything too physical like running or jumping, take some time off school to give your brain a chance to heal.

So, there I was: a 15-year-old girl who loved going to school, was in multiple dance classes and sports, who played in the band and enjoyed jumping on the trampoline, and suddenly I was told I wasn't allowed to do any of those things because of a brain injury. It felt like my entire life had been turned upside-down, and it sucked.

When I was finally able to go back to school for full days, I was relieved because things would *finally* get back to normal, right? Wrong again.

While I was away from school on my neurologist's orders, I had been having many conversations with a girl who was supposedly one of my closest friends. Turned out she had been...well, let's call it 'busy'. She was one of the people with whom I had conversations with over the course of the three months I was away from school. I told her everything that was going on and how I felt about it, and she seemed to understand and be there for me. At least, that's what I thought. What actually happened, was so much different.

This girl had managed to convince almost the entire senior high classes (picture a really close-knit group of people, maybe 60 kids from grades 10-12 combined) that I was faking it to get attention. Now, I'm having multiple emotions that are coursing through me as I'm writing this, and none of them are warm fuzzy feelings.

It's been almost a full year since I've seen this girl, but just knowing she played such a huge part in my anxiety and depression makes me upset to this day, and I'm not sure if I'll ever be able to fully get over that. When I went back to school, there were two people in my class who would talk to me. The rest, even close friends, had decided there wasn't anything wrong with me, and why would they think otherwise? They couldn't physically *see* a problem, so I must be fine, right?

Time for some facts. Concussions occur when your brain bounces and twists around inside your skull and hitting hard surfaces. This causes the extremely delicate cells inside your brain to stretch and damage. If you have a concussion, you've been hit hard enough in the head for your brain to move and smash into your skull. Because this happens *inside* your head, you never actually *see* anything, but does that mean it didn't happen? Does that mean you aren't injured? Of course not!

Concussions happen very frequently. Between 1.7 and two million people deal with them every year. Half of that number go undiagnosed and therefore, untreated. I was one of the lucky fifty per cent who had mine diagnosed and was able to make the lifestyle changes I needed, to reduce the ill effects. Even so, the impact it's had on my life has been insane.

It has been really hard for me going through all of this and there are parts I'm still dealing with today. There are times when I wish I could go back in time and change what happened to me because even though I've learned to accept this is who I am now, some days I wish it wasn't.

There has been *some* good that came out of my situation. With migraines, the only things I could do that didn't make it worse were reading, art, and crafts. I've blown through novel after novel, series after series, because it provided me an escape for those days when I was really down. I've also been able to develop my art skills. Art is one of my biggest passions, from drawing to painting to junk journaling. I'm blessed to have been given talent to be able to do these things because it also gives me an escape. There are times when I've been painting for hours and not even realized it, and I think that's an amazing thing. Everyone should have one hobby that gives them relief from reality once in a while.

I didn't foresee my concussion and the domino effect it has had on my life, just as I can't foresee what's in my future. The only thing I know is I *have* a future, and I would love my future to include traveling, namely to Italy!

I want you to know that while you might be stuck in a rut right now, things will get better. I didn't think they would, but here I am! In high school, I felt like the world and everyone in it was ugly for so many reasons, but being a survivor of a concussion and an awful high school experience and being able to channel my negative feelings into artwork has helped me to realize that although we have to look for it sometimes, there's beauty in the world, too.

By Victoria Moon, but I usually go by Tori.
I'm an eighteen-year-old girl living in Alberta, Canada. I managed to get this far, even with my constant nattering with my three brothers. I have many passions: art, photography, music, baking and decorating. If it's something art or craft oriented, chances are I'll love it! I've done a bit of

traveling, but I would absolutely love the chance to go back to Italy. This opportunity is the window to another dream of mine- writing a book. I'm so thankful that my cousin gave me a chance. Thank you, Kelly!

****

Oh No, Not My Hair!

By Elizabeth MacArthur

"You need to change your red hair. If you dyed your hair a different color, the boys would like you better. Then maybe you'd get a date."

These words landed on me with a big thud! I was in grade seven at the time. I was having a hard enough time fitting in and adjusting to the new junior high school without this. I thought I had made some new friends, but apparently not! The girl that said this to me was one of those new friends. When she said *"You need to change your red hair, you need to dye your hair a different color,"* I was devastated and crushed by her words.

This was my hair color she was talking about. How could I change my hair color? That's the color I was born with. Did this mean there was something fundamentally wrong with me? Was I imperfect with this terrible flaw of red hair? How could she not like that part of me? This was a direct personal hit and the message was clear – people don't like me because I looked different. I had no idea what to do with this. It hurt me to my core. My self-esteem and confidence took a huge hit that day.

I quickly decided I no longer wanted to be her friend. I still remember going up to her while she was standing at her locker and telling her I did not like what she said and did not want to be her friend anymore.

But the damage had already been done and I had already internalized the message. This was just one more piece about me people didn't like. That wasn't the first time I had been teased or picked on because of my hair color. For most of my childhood I had been made fun of or picked on for a few different things, including my hair. Or at least that was the way I saw it.

Like everything else, I buried it deep inside and created the belief I had to show up as someone different in order to be liked or accepted. But I wasn't willing to dye my hair so I tried to work around that by changing what I could. I would tell others what I thought they wanted to hear or do what others wanted to do just to be included. When hanging out in a group, I would say very little so no attention would be drawn to me. It was a lonely existence.

In my twenties, I started wearing my hair quite short. In fact, so short that sometimes I looked like a boy. Looking back now, I believe that was my way of trying to get rid of the red hair.

I carried this with me for a very long time. It wasn't until I was in my thirties, I started to look at my life and ask questions like, "How come my life isn't turning out the way I thought it would?" At this point I was living in my parents' basement, single, no children and just surviving. This was not where I thought I would be in my thirties.

Then an opportunity presented itself, a defining moment happened that changed everything. A friend asked me to go with her for a psychic reading. The reader told me if I didn't start doing some emotional healing work on myself that I was headed down a very difficult path. That woke me up. I knew she was right.

I started with counseling and did that for about a year. Then I had an opportunity to attend a workshop called Personal Mastery. I immediately knew I had to go. I even remember crying in the car on the way there and not knowing why. I walked into that workshop on Friday night and left Sunday night a different person. What I learned about myself in that weekend laid the groundwork for the rest of my healing journey. I was hooked on this alternative mode of healing. I continued with that personal development company for about three years attending and re-attending their workshops as often as I could. My self-esteem and confidence was increasing, I was feeling much better about myself and learning to love myself again.

But I didn't stop there! I started reading books. I would go to the bookstore, stand in front of the self-help section and look at the books until one jumped out at me. That was the next one I would read.

The next opportunity that showed up was a numerology reading. During this reading she talked about Lightworkers. I was not familiar with that term so I researched and found some books on the subject. I then took some courses from Doreen Virtue which provided me with more tools to use for my healing journey. This was the beginning of my introduction to energy work and understanding what energy work was.

The next opportunity that presented itself was through a healing modality called Family Constellation. I have done seven full constellations for myself and have been a representative for close to 500 constellations of others.

The next opportunity that came my way was in the form of forgiveness...Radical Forgiveness. Colin Tipping's book, 'Radical Forgiveness' showed up for me. While I was reading this book, I was connecting some of the next pieces of my healing journey.

I was so fascinated with the book I wanted to know if this process actually worked. At that time there were no coaches in my area so I opted to do an online program. I picked an issue I wanted to do some forgiveness on and I ran it through the online program. I was amazed at the results I got. I could feel that stuck energy trapped inside my victim story being released and transformed. It worked!

I wanted more of this Radical Forgiveness work. I researched the coaching certification program and made a decision to do the training, first for my own healing, and secondly as an option for a coaching business. My forgiveness healing continued.

The next opportunity that presented itself was the Akashic Records Healing/Practitioner course. I was introduced to this by having a reading done for myself. Then I read the book, 'How To Read The Akashic Records' by Linda Howe and immediately knew that I needed to add this to my own tool box and my coaching practice. Learning how to read my own Akashic Records is helping to deepen my own forgiveness work and coaching. It is quickly becoming another favorite tool.

Radical Forgiveness and the Akashic Records continue to be among the top healing tools I still use today. They have allowed me to forgive others as well as myself, which was one of the reasons why I had not been able to fully love myself and to realize I am beautiful regardless.

I'm not exactly sure when it happened, but somewhere throughout my healing work I transformed that belief of I was not pretty and my red hair was a hindrance. And when that happened, things changed. I started getting compliments on the color of my hair. Some people assumed it was dyed and ask me what dye color I used. When I told them it was my natural color, it was all mine, they were greatly disappointed and even envious, because they knew it could not be duplicated.

And even today with that little bit of natural grey highlights that run through my hair, I still get people complimenting me on my beautiful hair color and are envious when I tell them it does not come from a bottle! But even if I didn't have people telling me that, I now love my hair color and I feel beautiful!

I would like to leave you with this thought. I know it is never too late to do your own healing work in order to recognize your own beauty. Realizing your own beauty is far more powerful and enlightening than what anyone else thinks or says.

I encourage you to include Radical Forgiveness and Akashic Records healing in your own journey and to continue your incredible journey with courage and commitment. The results you will obtain are far beyond anything you can imagine today and is well worth the work and struggle to get there.

I never dreamt that I could feel this great about myself and I know I'm not done yet! I am forever grateful for making the decision and commitment to do my own healing work. I am also incredibly grateful for all the modalities and the people who showed up to support me in my healing journey. A very special heartfelt love and thank-you goes out to all.

As a Radical Living Master Coach and an Akashic Records Certified Healing / Advanced Practitioner, I am honored and humbled to be able to be of service to those who are on their healing journey and support you in whatever way I can.

*By **Elizabeth Macarthur** - Award winning Radical Living Master Coach, Akashic Records Certified Healing / Advanced Practitioner, and International Best-Selling Author, Elizabeth has worked with some of the top experts in the field to refine and enhance her own skills as a coach and practitioner.*

Elizabeth specializes in using both the Radical Forgiveness tools (a concept that is "radically" different from mainstream forgiveness), and the Akashic Records tools with her clients. This particular combination supports her clients in receiving powerful results with releasing their own blocks/issues and freeing themselves from more of their identification with "victim" stories, and the ensuing cycle of self-sabotaging patterns. Now they can manifest the life they truly desire with more love, abundance, inner peace, success and happiness.

Elizabeth also works with individuals who struggle with food issues. Drawing on her own success using the tools above, Elizabeth created a program that addresses the twin triggers associated with yo-yo dieting and overeating: the emotional pulls associated with unresolved past issues and the physical craving and addictions associated with our current food system. Her clients are being empowered to make healthier food choices resulting in better health, weight release and sustainability.

For more information, visit www.BreakThroughsAbounding.com or book your Discovery Call today to discuss how Elizabeth can support you on your journey at https://schedule-today.as.me/.

****

Escape from Food Guilt

By Karen Schaible

When I was eight-years-old, I first discovered food as a means of comfort and escape. I would sneak food into my hiding places and eat it whenever I had any feelings of sadness or loneliness. This was the start of my binge eating. From this young age, I was aware that I was the fat kid at school and felt like I would never fit in. By the beginning of grade three, I felt so much different than everyone else and had begun to dislike the person I was.

By the time I hit my teenage years, I was being bullied because of my weight and it only led to me feeling uglier. I felt so ashamed of myself and I was very unhappy. They even nicknamed me Chipmunk because I had big chubby cheeks. I did everything I could to stay in the shadows and not be noticed.

By the time I reached my last year of high school, I had still never been on a date and I had a strong desire to meet a guy who would date me. Because I had such a low level of self-esteem, self-confidence and self worth, I decided that if I wasn't skinny, I would never get a date.

That was the beginning of restrictive diets and over-exercising. I thought that I felt beautiful and accepted, being so successful I had lost 50 pounds in three months. I thought my life would be wonderful after that. It was then that I also went on my first date. Unfortunately, I also discovered I was still no happier or felt any better about myself than I had before I lost the weight. I had lost the weight on the outside but on the inside, I still felt fat.

After high school, I really got into partying and felt I needed a guy to make me feel special. I wanted to be skinny and beautiful, but that only led to further yo-yo dieting, over-exercising and binge eating. Because of my low self-esteem, I sought out unhealthy relationships and that made me feel even lower about myself.

At 21 I met a guy who gave me the attention I thought I wanted and needed to make me feel loved and beautiful. I still considered myself to be unattractive and undesirable. In a matter of six months, I was engaged and ten months later we were married. I said 'yes' to the marriage, not because of a deep love for him, but because my childhood dream was being fulfilled. Ever since I was a child, I thought if I was ever going to get married and have kids, I would only have one chance at this. That is how low my self-esteem was at that time.

That low self-esteem, lack of confidence plus being so uncomfortable about my body, kept me in a 22-year marriage to someone who was very emotionally abusive. I allowed myself to be completely manipulated because I had no idea what healthy boundaries were like.

Being in that marriage only made me feel more worthless. Because I was in such a dysfunctional marriage, my negativity and damaging self-talk led me back to my trusted friend — food. I should have been happy; I had three wonderful children, yet I was more depressed then ever. All I wanted to do was hide from the world.

I had missed out on so much with my children. At this time, my son was struggling with ADHD. I put all my effort into helping him and finding something that worked. Despite being a nurse, I went completely against the traditional medication his doctor advised and found a naturopath instead. Within the next six months, we had completely changed his diet along with natural treatments. This led to an amazing improvement in his behaviour.

It was then that I also discovered and developed my true passion for learning how food can heal, and how to eat for a healthy body, yet I still relied on old habits.

By the age of 41, I had a physical and mental breakdown. I was sick, exhausted, nauseated and couldn't eat. Again I lost 50 pounds, but this time in six weeks. I put a lot of stress on myself to be skinny and by restricting my food intake, indulging in binge eating, over-exercising, plus the stress of an unhealthy marriage, my health deteriorated.

I refused to listen to how stressed my inner self was and this was my body's way of crying out to get my attention and love. I was deep in the throes of depression and anxiety throughout my marriage. Up until that point, although on the outside it looked like I had it all together, I didn't want to keep on living this way anymore and I wanted to end my life. It was at this point my mind took over and I finally decided to stop it all.

Over the course of all those years, I tried every diet I could get my hands on. I had lost and gained 50 or more pounds at least six times, only to gain more of it back each time. I followed my diets to a T during the week, only to binge eat on everything in sight on the weekends. It was all or nothing. I beat myself up for the binge eating and thinking I had no will power. I cancelled plans to go out with friends or go to parties because I felt so fat or I didn't think I could control what I would eat.

Trying on new clothes in stores was so painful, I would wind up devastated and crying. I asked myself, "How can I love myself when I don't look anything like what the world says is beautiful?" I was stuck in a culture obsessed with food and the ideal body image. I walked around with a deep sense of shame, hoping I would eventually find the magic pill or diet to make me perfect.

I spent years starving myself, depriving myself, and hating myself. I thought if I just fit into a certain size, if my weight were at a certain number, if I had a certain image, I would be worthy.

If I could take back all the years I wasted on what other people thought, I would. Sometimes I think of how much I could have accomplished if I had only known how perfect I was already. Because of this, I missed out on so much with friends, my kids and myself. I was so obsessed with worrying about what others would think or say about me.

I knew at that time, there was also a higher power looking out for me. I decided I was going to get better physically and then focus on myself. I would let go of putting all my energy into saving my marriage and giving to everyone else. I worked hard on pulling myself out of that dark place. For the first time in years, I started saying yes to myself. I put all my energy into personal growth by doing the inner work of learning that I had feelings. I let the emotions come up I previously numbed, denied and pushed down for most of my life, this time without turning to food.

Having started the inner work of slowly building up my self-confidence and self-esteem, next on my list was dealing with my marriage. I was now able to see I lived with someone who did not have my best interests at heart and who emotionally abused me worse than I did to myself. This was not the way I wanted to live the rest of my life. Ultimately, leaving a 22-year marriage was one of the hardest decisions I had ever made, but was also the best decision to finally treat myself like I was worth it.

I spent enough time focusing on doing and saying what I thought others wanted, rather than with what resonated with me. I had lost touch with myself because it was all filtered through what I thought others would or should see. At that time, it was all about what I looked like on the outside. I resolved what people think about my looks and about me was not more important than being who I am meant to be.

Over the next eight years, as I continued to heal my relationship with myself and to dig deeper into my self-discovery I was finally able to lose the last 50 pounds and keep it off except for the last 10 to 15 pounds. This was because there was still something inside of me that was holding me back. I was not quite there yet.

I was still falling back into my old habit of restrictive dieting and over-exercising and instead of turning to food, now I was turning to alcohol. I loved the taste of red wine; at least that is what I told myself. With all the personal development I had done, I also had the awareness this was not the struggle I wanted to continue with. I decided to attend AA and had completely stopped drinking for 14 months. It was during those months I was completely able to practice vulnerability and integrity with others and myself. At this time, I also started working with a life coach who helped me get to know myself like I had never done before. I was taught to question old thoughts and beliefs that were preventing me from losing the weight and keeping it off.

As well, by becoming aware of those beliefs, I was able to build the self-confidence, self-love and self-esteem I had not had since I was a very young child. I was done with filling the void in my feelings with food and then with alcohol because I didn't want — or know how — to feel. I learned how to accept and love all my feelings, even the 'bad' ones like anger, fear and shame. I had decided I truly wanted to enjoy my life.

Today, my life is more than I ever imagined it could be. It is not perfect and I still have my struggles but now I have the ability to cope with them in a healthy way without using food or alcohol. Yes, I can still have days where negative body image creeps up on me, but those days are few and far between. When they do come, they don't have power over me like they used to do because now I have the tools that allow me to connect with my body and shift my thinking.

I have learned to feel my feelings and then release them, but this is still a work in progress. I thank the universe I could deal with the depression and anxiety that consumed me, and I did it without the need for medication, food or alcohol to get me through it. I continue to work on letting go of mind chatter that says, "I am not good enough." I am done with being stuck in the cycle of dieting, over exercising and binge eating. Issues with food and body image no longer hold me back.

I have learned how to lose weight naturally without counting calories or excess exercising. I have developed the awareness required to stop the emotional eating. I still do exercise and only because I want to do it and it feels good, not because I feel compelled to do it. I love my body, instead of feeling shame and guilt about it and about myself. I eat what feels good and not what is good or bad food. Food and weight no long rule my life.

I am so passionate about helping other women break free from the cycle of yo-yo dieting, obsessive exercise, binge eating and body shaming. I love helping them get to a place where they are eating healthy foods and taking care of themselves and discovering real freedom and peace around food and their bodies.

When you heal your inner self and have a sense of self-love, self-acceptance, self-worth and inner beauty, you will no longer need to turn to food to numb out any feelings. When this happens and you have your true beauty radiating from the inside, you will lose the weight without a struggle and keep it off permanently.

Karen Schaible is a Weight Transformation and Body Image Coach for women who have spent too many years dieting, binge eating and hating their bodies. A weight loss coach helping women to lose weight from the inside out. Karen spent 25 years battling her body, yo-yo dieting, suffering with binge eating, anxiety and depression. Through working with life coaches and a deep dedication to learning and growing in changing what was not working in her life, she was able to get off all medication, stop obsessing over food and exercise, and lose 100 pounds by healing her inner self and love of her body.

Karen was a Registered Nurse for 27 years working in many areas of nursing but mainly Psychiatry, Home Care and the Bariatric Clinic. She ran a Nutritional Consulting Clinic and worked alongside Dietitians and Nutritionists. She is a Certified Eating Psychology Coach and is currently training to be a Certified Weight Loss and Life Coach by Brook Castillo with The Life Coach School. She is married, has three grown children and one adorable granddaughter. www.KarenSchaible.com

****

How My Life's Work Has Made People Feel Beautiful

By Rachel Gour

I never understood why or how this career came to me, but truly I wanted to do it even though I didn't feel beautiful.

I wanted to be the one that had the best hair, the newest look and the heads that turned.

How did this career fill my soul like no other? Over the years I found out I wasn't the only one who felt this way .... it was a common feeling!

I have heard it all, every single client starts with a negative aspect; "I don't like..... about my hair."

I always ask "What do you like about your hair?" and surprisingly this turns it around.

I have had some women who believe beauty is only skin deep, but as I learn more about them, they are the souls of Beauty. Every human being

I have touched has been a beautiful individual and I see things so much deeper than my eyes, it's the story of their journey they have traveled.

I began this journey of beauty 30 years ago. Learning about the beauty within the souls I have touched, this has been the best gift.... I believe as woman we need to celebrate the beautiful beings we are, take care of the person we are with and remind them of the things that make us attracted to each other with the souls within each of us. This is truly not celebrated enough and I do try my hardest, woman to woman to be the one that spreads the beauty of you!

Beauty is a billion dollar business and its on every corner, every moment of our existence; from street signs to groceries to TV ads and so on, but when you get personal with a person in your chair, you can touch the soul of a person and bring out the beauty within.

Years ago when I was in school, I met a girl who had been given a path like no one I had known. She was burnt as a child and I saw her as a person who was different and unique. I knew in my life this would happen again and again, that I would meet people who where gifted. I would never let people not understand the gift she had been given and it was not our job to criticize or make fun. I wanted to know the soul of why.

Over my many years, I began to know this person deeper and deeper and never once saw the scars as negative or the way someone else for the first time would see her without understanding the gifts this person had been given!

One day I found myself in a situation as an adult when I had to defend and protect her. I was shocked and stunned at first and grateful she had missed this individual's words. I was not going to allow this to change our day! I was however, going to make sure this woman never say something so cold and ugly to another human being.

I stepped in said my piece and proceeded to keep the day fun and exciting as we were on a girls' shopping trip.

It forever changed me in understanding that beauty had taken us too far. That some people had been so convinced our outside beauty was our only asset. I knew my work had to change and I had to never fixate on anyone's negativity and consciously get people to understand the gifts they had been given; lived higher and stronger within them.

I am forever grateful to my friend and our friendship... this woman makes beauty shine, she takes beauty within to the next level because her journey shows me and many others that beauty is not skin deep, it's within all of us.

I am grateful for the path of beauty; it has impacted my life. I get to see the beauty in everyone and touch individuals for who they truly are everyday!

My life as hairdresser has been my blessing in life and I'm so glad I met Kelly, the beautiful burned girl in my story. You may or may not have guessed by now, but Kelly is the one who I defended. I am forever grateful to my friend Kelly and to our friendship... this woman makes beauty shine, she takes beauty within to the next level because her journey shows me and many others that beauty is not skin deep it's with in all of us.

Rachel Gour has been a hairstylist for 30 years. She has exceptional clientele and is excited to travel the world in the hair industry. Rachel has also done hair for both of Kelly's documentaries, SexAbility and Still Beautiful plus other feature films. Her family is her first love with two sons and extended family members who mean the world to her. My life is a blessing as is my friends and family!
www.HairByRachel.ca

****

Dear Precious One, It's not your fault!

By Madie Vilbig-King

You did not cause this to happen, nor could you have controlled it! But you can control what you do going forward. And go forward, you MUST! You, and only you, can control how this incident affects your life! I want you to lead a happy life! A life rich in joy and loaded with success, in spite of, and especially because of, what has happened to you! That will be your greatest revenge! But do not do it out of revenge, do it for you. Because you are worth it, you are beautiful and you deserve it!! Unfortunately, bad things do happen to good people.... and life is frequently unfair! You have been brutalized, but do not take on the role of a victim! You have been victimized, but you must choose to be victorious!

I would like to share with you some of the trials and atrocities of my life I had to overcome so I could have happiness and success! Then I'll share with you what I have learned to help you with your journey to a rewarding life.

I was adopted by wonderful loving parents when I was only seven-days-old. They had a four-year-old son they adopted also. Instantly, he was always getting in trouble for waking me. I took time and attention away from him which of course, he wasn't happy about and promptly began asking to send me back! Everyone, Mom and Dad, and the entire extended family, all seemed to think this was cute and funny, everyone but me! Their laughter encouraged his resentful behavior. It wasn't long before he would hit me when no one was looking. When I was four or five he knocked my two front teeth out! He even tried to drown me twice before I was eight! Why did he hate me so?

Life was chaotic and confusing! My Dad travelled for work a lot. Mom worked too, cared for us and ran the house. She was frequently very stressed and struggled to deal with it all. I had to be good so Mom would not cry!

Finally, Dad was home more and Mom was so happy! My brother and I were growing up, both of us were in school. I did very well in school, but my brother did not. He was really smart, so nobody could understand why his grades were so bad. There was a lot of yelling at home because he was getting into trouble at school. The Nuns at the Catholic school were mean to him and in turn he was meaner to me! Eventually he was sent to a psychiatrist and put on some medication. And at some point, it was determined he was also suffering from dyslexia. That explained a lot about his bad grades and acting out! Meanwhile, he had gotten better at hiding his meanness, so when I tried to complain, I was told not to be a tattletale! Are people allowed to hurt me? Isn't someone going to protect me?

Mom and Dad were very socially active and soon we were old enough they would leave me in in my brother's care while they went out at night. Sometimes he would leave too and other times he would have his friends over.

It was two weeks before my eleventh birthday, when I was awakened with a male on top and inside of me.

There was blood on me and my pajamas the next morning. My Mom determined I must have started my period and it was not mentioned again.

Almost over night, my brother was sent away to a boarding school. It was calm and happy in our home now and I liked that, but oddly I did miss my brother.

When he came home after two semesters, part of me was glad he was home.... there was lots going on again and I was bored.

Well, I guess I must have been a pest or something, because the meanness began again. This is when I discovered alcohol and cigarettes, I think I was 12 or 13. I didn't drink daily, just when Mom and Dad would have parties. I felt euphoric when I drank and was able to forget the unpleasantness.

Soon I was beginning to be quite cute and lots of boys liked me! My brother would be mean to them and run them off! I didn't understand that. He said he was protecting me. Protecting me from what?

When I was 15 he got married. Life was good during my high school years. I had lots of boyfriends, lots of friends, lots going on and I fell in love!

I was still drinking on occasion and after a year of being in love, I began having an intimate relationship with my boyfriend. I didn't know why my 'first' time was so easy. My boyfriend wondered why I didn't have any bleeding. I had no answer. I wrote it off to horseback riding or something. I had no memory of anything else that could have altered my physiology.

During my first year of college, I came home for spring break and went out with some of my friends. On our way home, we stopped by my friend's boyfriend's apartment, he wasn't alone. He started hitting my friend! No one else did anything, so I jumped in between them. Then the fight got very bad... I was severely beaten, many broken bones, mostly in my face. I had to have surgery on my nose and my ruptured ear drum.

My drinking escalated after this and throughout my college years, as did my sexual promiscuity. I now believed that sex was how to get a man to love me, and I was desperate to be loved. I would tolerate any treatment and now had a high tolerance to mistreatment. I had begun to believe I was not valuable. Some memory from my childhood was creeping into my conscious awareness and it frightened me. I couldn't understand these little snippets of a memory. It was a very confusing time. And of course, my grades suffered, so I had to sit out a semester. I rented a house with a couple of other girls and got a job.

My first boss was creepy. He was about 20 years my senior. I did not like him and hated the job. It was a junk resale shop, and everything was nasty and dirty, just like him! I needed the money and I had no real skills. One day, we had to work late and he took me to dinner. While driving me back to my car, I got very dizzy and things got fuzzy and he refused to take me home.... And then it happened. He raped me. I don't know what drug he had slipped me, but finally he took me back to my car, so I could 'go home to clean up before work'. I vowed he would never see me again, I didn't even go back for my last paycheck!

Then I found a job waiting tables in a bar. I made great money and was having fun again, so when my scholastic probation was lifted I enrolled in some classes, but was not particularly interested in college. With all the drinking and not taking good care of myself, I became deathly ill and my family came and moved me back home. I didn't even get the chance to say good bye to anyone! Leaving that environment probably saved my life, as my kidneys were shutting down! My aunt and uncle were doctors so their care pulled me through again. (I say again because I almost died from hepatitis and mononucleosis at age five, and pneumonia at sixteen!

As soon as I got well, my Dad insisted that I go back to school! He told me that I should go to nursing school. He didn't leave room for objections or discussion! He was serious and I knew it!

Surprisingly, I loved nursing school and made the Dean's list. Got a great job at a top hospital and bought my first house before I graduated! I was on top of the world!

But soon the demons returned! I'm not sure what triggered the nightmares, but it was the memory of that night! The memory of several nights! I found myself drinking heavily, daily! I was working 3-11, so my career was not affected when I would sleep it off every morning, but my personal life was a mess!

In my twenties, I got arrested for DWI twice and I had had an abortion. One night I was hijacked out of my car by a man with a gun! He pistol whipped me in the head and had every intention of raping me, but the noise of our struggle drew the attention of a wonderful couple who ran my attacker off! Now I was even afraid to leave my house after dark! I was terrified every night coming home from work!

A friend of mine said one sentence to me that made a huge difference, "He controlled you for a period of time and that was awful, I know, but are you gonna let him control the rest of your life?" Wow! I made a decision right then that I wanted to be in charge of me and my life!

Not knowing what to do or how to help myself, I finally went to a counselor at age 28.

It was while I was seeing him the total knowledge of the details of all those horrible nights came flooding back to me! I Thank God I was already seeing a professional! I was filled with hurt, confusion and anger! I had totally suppressed those memories! This gentle psychologist helped me work through so much pain, confusion and anger! He showed me how I had been living without direction, too! And he even helped me get to a place of compassion, love and forgiveness for every member of my family, including myself and all the people who had hurt me!

So now, my career was flourishing and I had bought my third home! It was beautiful and I was too! I was happy and successful! And I was raped again, by my male house mate! And mugged again, this time it was just to rob me! Thank God! But now, when these awful things happened, I was armed with better coping skills. Now I was not destroyed, nor completely powerless.

Facing it all, grieving the losses and hurts were an important step to my healing process. Journaling and writing a timeline helped! It was equally important to take ownership and responsibility for my life. You are not always responsible for what happens to you, but maybe you played some part, large or small, in how it became possible for you to be where you were, so that it could happen! Or maybe not! But either way, you need to know, as you may have to adjust your behavior, or change your decisions to have the life you seek.

I have come to peace with the past and while I am not happy all this has happened, I can see the parts that I had a hand in and how it all gave me something. Strength, wisdom, a voice, insight, determination... even compassion.

During these last 34 years of my life I had struggles and strife, and major hurts and heartaches. I had two marriages and two divorces. I had a miscarriage, then was blessed to have given birth to a 10-week premature child and shortly thereafter, became a single parent. I have been confronted with health issues that altered my life. Death of loved ones that changed the trajectory of my life. I have faced extreme financial hardship and have even lost two homes. I have woken up with fire on three sides of me that destroyed my business and 32 others! But feel blessed and grateful to be alive!

I have been lied to and stolen from by loved ones and strangers alike! I have been used and abused and have even abused myself!

I have given up my career and home to live with and take care of my Mom. I have started several businesses and learned about failure! And in recent years, I have gained weight, but by the same token, I have had extreme joys and satisfactions! I have learned new skills and disciplines. I have learned the importance of having healthy boundaries! And my family has grown! Most importantly, I have come to know and believe I am worthy of, and can have, whatever magnificent life I choose to live, as long as I am willing to put in the effort to attain it!

What keeps me going is daily prayer, meditation and my faith in a loving God who wants only the best for me! Also, the awareness and decision I made that night so long ago, when I declared I was in control, co-creating the life I want! I had allowed myself to flounder around without true purpose or real goals. I had begun to believe falsehoods about myself and others.

And occasionally, I drift into that same complacency and that's when the demons always resurface! Therefore now, I regularly check-in with myself. I regularly decide what I desire for my life; I plan and go for it! I write down my vision for my life and set the goals that will get me there, then I plan my days accordingly. I make myself and my intentions my priority!

It is my life and I get to be in charge of it! I do not drink as I once did, I no longer need to, nor do I smoke any more. I control the thoughts in my head and I choose what enters my head, such as the things I hear, see and read! I choose what success and happiness look like for me! My associations and my actions are deliberate now. I read a lot of books, go to seminars and continually seek to improve my mind, my skills and my attitude! I live my life intentionally, with direction, purpose and intentions!

I forgive myself for my poor judgement of the past, and I forgive others theirs. I love myself even though I am not as young and pretty as I once was. And I love others too! I believe, to have a glorious life, even during the mundane or difficult times, you must do these things! Be kind and caring to yourself and others for there is much joy in having compassion and giving to others!

Godspeed Loved One! You are in my prayers for you are, as I am, still beautiful!

Madie Vilbig-King is a mother to a grown son. She retired early from her first career as a RN after 30 yrs with multiple specializations, certifications and awards. Her proudest moment as a RN came as a result of working 25 years with HIV/AIDS patients and supervisor in the home care industry. She has been self-employed over 30 years in the medical industry, real estate and retail. She has served in various leadership roles for many charitable organizations including the Great Gluten Escape Camp. She is involved with developing people through her businesses and associations with the Slight Edge Mindset Mastery and the Pachamama Alliance Organization. She is also a certified facilitator of the Awaken the Dreamer symposium and Game Changer Intensive. She is passionate about health and healing.

****

The Journey is the Same for All of Us

By Shawn T. McIntyre

To develop a seeking that goes from living just on the surface of external things, stuff or appearances to the world of eyesight and outside patterns to developing a seeking that guides and directs inside into internal patterns of things, stuff and appearances in the forms called thoughts and emotions or feelings.

What is interesting to me from my experience in this journey of seeking, is the integrating process of 'truth' and how everything starts to become beautiful as truth reveals a gift of insight.

This is where I learned that with the right kind of eyesight - everything is beautiful; but it didn't start out that way for me. You see, I grew up being bullied, ridiculed and laughed at. In school I felt as though I was stupid. I remember kids in class laughing at me when I was called on to stand up and give answers to questions asked from my teacher. I didn't know it at the time, but the way my mind worked was that I was already operating off INSIGHT. Whether I was reading a text book, story or watching the mouth move on the teacher, I would hear and perceive my own meanings. The challenge was when I had to give an answer; it wasn't the exact words or answer the teacher or other students would get. I got laughed at and learned to shut down this insight and tried to fit in operating off EYESIGHT to be like everyone else and avoid the feelings and thought of disconnect. It wasn't a beautiful feeling.

This wasn't a mistake though; as I learned valuable skills to read my environment of people, places, things and events. It also started to grow a disconnect inside and the more I tried to fit in on the outside, the more pain and struggle it created internally. I could run and hide from the truth that there was something more and deeper called an inside world and it needed my attention.

By the time I was in high school, I managed to survive the ridicule of growing up feeling stupid and not good enough both at home and alone, but it had taken its toll; because by the time I was sixteen I was severely under weight, extreme acne, braces and glasses...talk about a picture of beauty. NOT!

Right on time for the period of life where a real social life mattered! In fact, I would wear more than one shirt and pants to try and look bigger so I wouldn't get bullied or made fun of or to try again to fit in and feel accepted.

I was alone which really made me feel ugly and stupid and I just wanted to hide myself. Yet all I really wanted was to not feel alone anymore.

I didn't realize it but, these insights were 'gifts' - gifts given so real, freedom and power that resided on the inside could be developed so no person, place, thing or event could say or do anything to hold me back. I didn't know it, but I was body building. Building the strength through resistance training to create a physical body, a mental body and emotional body that could withstand any conditions that would come my way. I didn't know it at the time, but I can see and relate to how a caterpillar becomes a butterfly. Nothing was wrong, it was all purposeful to a deeper more powerful creation and version of 'me'.

When the outside and inside structures were developed, something amazing happened! There was a greater capacity for something deep inside to flow out. I now see, for this incredible powerful UNSTOPPABLE person to emerge, I had to go through these messy situations. And they were all gifts to experience a peace and power I call True Power that the

ALONE feeling was transformed into ALL-One. This state of ONENESS is beauty.

Beauty is where you come from, not what you try and make yourself to look like or even feel like. Oneness stopped the proving that I needed to fit in or look a certain way to be happy or worthy or to feel beautiful. By going all in - to know thyself, I discovered I can find beauty amongst the ashes that I have ALWAYS BEEN BEAUTIFUL.

Eyesight to insight and with the right kind of perception, no matter what you look like, it is amazing. There is energy and aliveness and this aliveness is what strikes a different cord or frequency and today I am a Pro Fitness Model that has been on covers of fitness magazines and judged on my appearance.

To many outsiders, they think it is about looking good, to feel good, but I know more than that, or should I say deeper than that. I do not say beauty is skin deep or the inside is where real beauty is. Beauty is the seeking of who you truly are in the inside so your perception goes from 'eyesight' to 'insight'; where you look at yourself with love, compassion, amazement and a deep knowing of a power within!

We all have this ability to rise and be beautiful and go for what is in our hearts! That is beautiful!

Shawn T. McIntyre is the founder and CEO of UNSTOPPABLE EmpireTM, Workout of Your Life and Shawn T. McIntyre Fitness. He is a published author and corporate health and wellness trainer, professional fitness competitor (currently Top 10 World Beauty Fitness Fashion North American Champion) and international cover model.

When Shawn started his career as a fitness model, he focused solely on his appearance while other aspects of his life suffered drastically, including his business, relationships and overall well-being. Through years of tribulation he finally recognized the need for a total personal transformation.

With his personal achievements being met, in-turn Shawn has been helping and inspiring others to achieve their own personal transformation with clarity and power – not fear. Through education, on the benefits of physical and mental well-being, he coaches clients to help

them achieve success in business, fitness and life by being
UNSTOPPABLE. ShawnM.Fit@Gmail.com

****

Cancer is NOT Taking Me Out!

By Sylvie van Steenoven

My name is Sylvie van Steenoven, I am a seven-time cancer survivor! At the time of writing this, I am actually going through my eighth diagnosis with a brand new tumour to my front left lobe in my head.

In 2005 at the age of 35 I was diagnosed with breast cancer. Two very small tumors were found at the time, no lymphatic involvement so stage 0.

In November of 2005 which was a couple weeks after learning about my diagnosis, I had a lumpectomy to remove the tumors and the surrounding tissue around it along with lymph nodes. Unfortunately, the pathology results from that lumpectomy led to not having clear margins, which means when they take out and test the outer areas of what they removed, there was cancer cells in that area.

So now we're left with a dilemma, do we do another lumpectomy, take out a little bit more and see if we can remove the rest of the cancerous cells? Or do we just opt to do a mastectomy and then remove the breast completely and hope it will remove all the cancer completely? All things that needed to get done quickly with no time to really think about what you do or don't do because you're made to think your decisions need to be made ASAP.

I decided instead of doing another lumpectomy and having the possibility of not having clear margins, I opted to do the mastectomy. The beginning of December 2005 I went in to have a mastectomy of my right breast. Again, we removed more lymph nodes to make sure there was no lymphatic involvement. This time two lymph nodes came back questionable, so what does that mean questionable?

I mean after all is it there or is it not, there's no inbetween! The great thing about having surgery in December is that it was my year to host Christmas dinner, so I got to sit and watch everyone make Christmas dinner around me while I got to milk it all during Christmas time! LOL

Now with questionable lymph node involvement, we need to decide what do we do because having two lymph nodes that are questionable means it has traveled or could have traveled to other areas outside of the breast. I am offered chemotherapy, which to me was extreme considering I had just done the extreme decision and removed my entire breast. I asked why they were referring me to have 15 rounds of chemotherapy?

Their answer, are you sitting down? Their answer was because I was young enough and I could take it! No word of a lie, exact words from my Oncologist. This of course did not sit well with me at all and I wanted a second opinion which also doesn't sit well with Oncology Department but it's my body and I'm going to do to it what I want!

Then from the second Oncologist I am told I could have a different approach; I could be on tamoxifen for five years which is a hormone drug. Now let me just state from the pathology results were now ER PR positive, which means estrogen receptor-positive and progesterone receptor positive. In 'you and me' language that means the cancer is feeding off of my hormones, so we need to deal with the hormone issue, thus the idea for Tamoxifen. So now I'm reading like a mad woman to find out what are the pros and cons of taking it.

After walking around with only one breast for a year and it was making me a little bit uncomfortable; I couldn't wear the fake ones, they just weren't comfortable. They were hot, they didn't sit in the bra properly, they just were not for me. I asked to see a plastic surgeon. After going through all the discussions with the plastic surgeon, I decided a tram flap reconstruction was the way to go. February 2007 we do a 12-hour surgery! Yes you read that right 12 hours, I mean I fell asleep and woke up in two seconds, but my family waited for 12 hours.

Now you are probably wondering what would happen to your left breast, you didn't have that removed? In the surgery I did, so I removed the left breast and did tram flap reconstruction.

When I looked in the mirror I was a great big happy face! I had a scar which went from hip bone to hip bone, which is the smile from your mouth, I had my new belly button hole which was kind of like your nose and then the way the breasts are cut they are in the shape of eyes!

Every time I looked in the mirror naked, I am a great big happy face! At that time, I also didn't have nipples, so I wore stickers, yep stickers! I would wear hearts or stars or smiley faces or busses or whatever the heck I wanted to wear. Whatever the mood I was in, I was going to make this as fun as it could possibly be in such a horrible situation. And really, every time you look at yourself naked in your happy face how can you not be happy....... happy to be alive!!!

So yes now we are in 2009 and I'm newly diagnosed again ....first recurrence. We end up finding a clot in my subclavian vein which is one of the side effects of Tamoxifen, immediately I am stopped from taking Tamoxifen and I'm now on blood thinners. And now I'm thinking here we go again through chemotherapy again, through the radiation oncologist because that's what they want you to do.

I however, have a different idea. I am thinking with everything that I've been reading over the years and informing myself to make the best decisions for me, I was not going to go that route.

I found an alternative doctor in Los Angeles Dr Michael Galitzer who really resonates with me. We do a great big fundraiser and lo and behold off to Los Angeles we go. In February 2010 I meet the famous Dr. Galitzer and he has been my alternative doctor ever since! As I'm writing this, in four days I leave to go see him to find out what he has to say about this new tumor that has decided to test me yet again.

Instantly I have a connection to him and I know he is truly on my team and here to help me survive. I go home with a bunch of stuff to take, things to cut out, how to change my eating, how to start meditating, how to start with daily affirmations, how to reduce the stress in my life which are all things that are crucial to beating this disease in my opinion!!

Through all the ups and downs and it's a much longer to share, but in 2011 it decided to come back, I got rid of it, in 2012 it came back in the right breast and chest wall again and this time I opted to listen to them and do radiation now. I only had a couple of tumors on my right side. I do fifteen rounds of radiation and six months later I am now stage four and they are giving me three to six months to live and my lungs are full of tumors!

I'm thinking, how do I go from stage one because there's lymphatic involvement to doing radiation and only having two small tumors, now I am stage four terminal diagnosis three to six months to live? None of this made sense. All I knew was, after the initial fear, anger and sadness and all the emotions we are allowed to go through when you're on this journey, I told them to take their time limit and stick it where the sun doesn't shine!

I am a mother and a wife and I had too much stuff to do and I wasn't listening to their time limit that was given to me in August 2013. There has been a lot that has happened in between like 49 rounds of chemo, fifteen rounds of radiation, losing my hair, not having hair for three years but again for the sake of keeping this short and sweet I want to leave you with a few things.

Being diagnosed with cancer is one hell of a scary ride so I want you to read and read. I want you to inform yourself, I want you to know your options, I want you to know there isn't only one or two options, there's multiple options!! Yes you're going to feel bombarded, find someone that has walked this walk. It doesn't mean what I've done will work for you, it doesn't mean what worked for somebody else will work for other people but I will tell you this, and I believe this to the core of my being that if you sit and you do a countdown because they've given you a countdown, you will terminate at that countdown!!

I have seen it happen more times than I wish to share. You need to meditate, you need to de-stress, you need to find a circle of people that will not even necessarily agree with the choices you might make, but they have to respect your choices! It is your body, you are allowed to do whatever you wish in the way of treatment and in the way you choose to do this fight. Because if you choose the treatment that resonates with you, you have a better chance, I cannot stress that enough!!

I have been to so many clinics in the US over the years and I have learned that stress is the number one killer!! A big piece of the puzzle you need to believe and feel; you can beat it and then you do everything you can to do that! In love and health….Sylvie

Sylvie van Steenoven *48 years young mother of three boys, grandmother of two, seven-time cancer survivor, WBFF Transformation Finalist 2018. Born in Hull, Quebec in 1970. www.Healthiest-You.com*

****

Still Beautiful in a Cut-Throat World of Fashion

By Kelly Wollf

It took me years to make it — to be successful in the world of fashion. At least as others might define success. I managed a multitude of fashion stores across an entire district, making a corporate-level wage, working 80-90 hours per week, sacrificing health, relationships, and family to become the executive I had always longed to be, and to be respected in the industry. I was committed to this career, this life of long overtime hours, of excitement and stress, of beauty and expression. And I was good at it. Damn good at it.

My identity was as a fashion executive and God, how I loved my work. I loved every joyful and painful minute of it. I loved the life so much I willingly sacrificed almost everything for it. Yes, I sure loved it, all right.

But I loved my son more.

A painful, messy divorce wasn't enough; now I was fighting for custody of my boy, an innocent child caught up in the battles, anger, and confusion of an adult world.

I sat with my boss in the car, dabbing at the tears in my eyes, looking in the mirror and trying to compose myself, to erase the blush in my cheeks from crying. "I need to go see my lawyer this afternoon about my son," I said.

My boss stared straight ahead and was quiet for a moment. Then she turned to me, and in a voice empty of compassion, said, "Honey, what *I need* is for you to be committed to your job."

Committed to my job? If there was one thing I never expected to hear from my boss, it was that I needed to commit to my job. A veiled threat? No, not veiled. Overt. This was a real threat. My son...or my job. My boss didn't think I could handle both. What the hell was I going to say to that?

The corporate world of fashion leads us to believe that beauty exists within the domain of a particular body type. They would never say this out loud, of course, but consider that most corporate fashion outlets have one look, one body type, and one sizing model. They would love to take your money, but if the pants don't fit you, you can't buy their pants, and the message is, there's something wrong with you. The pants don't fit, so you don't fit into their notion of what is considered beautiful. And if you don't fit into their notion of what is considered beautiful, they don't want you wearing their clothes. Nobody considers that instead of there being something wrong with the customer, there might actually be something wrong with the pants. This simple misinterpretation of the fitting of a pair of pants can have a damaging effect on the self-image of girls and young women.

If the clothes don't fit, women feel there is something wrong with them. They can feel excluded. Alone. Ugly. And if you don't believe it, just listen to how some women talk about their bodies. There's a lot of trash talk. *Cellulite is showing. Bum is too big. Bad skin. Things are sticking out where they shouldn't be.* That kind of talk can break my heart.

We are still bombarded daily by advertising telling us what is beautiful, and most of us feel like we just don't measure up. We don't have the body shape the fashion industry identifies as 'ideal', we don't have the right face, the right lips, the right nose, the right — well, *anything*. Corporate fashion might have the noble goal of helping women feel beautiful, but when clothing is designed and produced around an 'ideal', many women are left feeling the exact opposite. The result is that we chase the feeling of being beautiful with Botox fillers, hair dye, Spanx, and push up bras, and while none of these is problematic in themselves, if they are not in alignment with our personal styles and true selves, they can hurt more than help.

It's not my goal here to demonize the world of corporate fashion. Lord knows I loved working in that world. And it has its place, but it's not for everyone. Corporate fashion makes it seem the formula for looking good is determined entirely by what we wear. But really, what we wear is only half of it. The other half is how we feel about ourselves, despite what we're wearing. We all know how a genuine smile all by itself can make someone beautiful and brighten up the room.

I'm not immune to the messages of beauty that are espoused by advertising, that make us feel like we're not quite measuring up, that cause us to open our purses in our desire to try to fit in. These messages affect us in the primal part of our brain – we want to belong – to be beautiful is to be important, and to be important is to belong. I get confused sometimes myself.

I've always loved fashion, ever since I was a little girl. Very quickly, I became the fashion consultant for my mother. We could never afford to buy the clothing that was in the popular stores at the time, but we had a sewing machine and my mother loved to sew more than anything. With my fashion ideas and her sewing skills, we were a dynamite team, both passionate about our respective roles. Sometimes we got carried away and Mom would be working away at her sewing machine while I yelled from the door that we had to get going because we were late for something. In a pinch, I would even back her car out of the driveway onto the street to save a few seconds. That was long before I actually had a license to drive.

Those years as a child and later as a teenager, designing clothes and experimenting with hundreds of different styles, were my formative years for a career in the fashion industry. I was a roly-poly, pudgy little kid, but I never felt like I needed to be slimmer in order to feel pretty. For me, fashion had never been about beauty. It had always been about expression. It didn't really matter what I had made for myself, if it wasn't in alignment with how I felt about myself, wearing it didn't make me feel beautiful.

We often get it backwards. We think wearing the right clothing will make us feel beautiful, turn us into something better than we are, more confident, better looking, and more professional. But it's more likely we'll feel beautiful, more confident, and more professional if we already see ourselves that way and then express it in a style that works for us.

Dressing well is an art form and it's important to me to help people express themselves in the way they want, to help them experiment with different looks and styles, and to feel beautiful regardless of what they're wearing. I want to know who the person is, where she was born, how old she is, what it was like for her growing up, and what her current challenges are.

The more I know about her, and the more she knows about herself, the better chance we have of helping her express it in the clothes she wears. There is nothing more thrilling than helping women find their styles because they transform right before my eyes. We both smile because we know we've just nailed it. It's so electrifying!

I was thinking about this as I sat in the car with my boss. Her demand for my unwavering commitment to my job was a moment of truth. Sure, it was about my son, but it was also about my truth as a champion of fashion. In the corporate fashion industry, I would forever be committed to the paradigm of 'one look, one body type, one sizing model'. My boss's ultimatum was an opportunity for me to change my life, to embrace my son and to become an ambassador for beauty, especially for those women who did not fit into the 'ideal'.

I didn't say anything to my boss right away. I just nodded my understanding and went to my lawyer to fight for my son's right for a balanced and happy life with both his mother and father. But it only took me two weeks to build my own business and open my first store in Edmonton's Old Strathcona. I called it C'est Sera Boutique and submitted my resignation to corporate fashion.

That was 18 years ago and I've never regretted giving up the corporate world that I loved so much. My philosophy hasn't changed since the beginning. My team of beauty ambassadors and I aim to help customers create wardrobes and outfits to match who they are. If the outfit doesn't work for a client, if it doesn't truly reflect who she is, I don't try to sell it to her. We keep working at it until we find something that *does* work.

Recently, I've even created my own brand – Kelly Wollf. The wolf in Kelly Wollf is mysterious, playful, sexy, and strong. I've surrounded myself with an amazing and wonderful team – 15 humans, one Scotsman (who is also a human), three dogs and of course, my mother, who enjoys sneaking up on unsuspecting new team members and saying, "Don't you know who I am?"

In case it isn't obvious, I've found my passion and I love to share it with others. To all the women reading this, if you have never had the permission to express yourself fully, I give that to you now. go for it! You deserve it! I'm not one for giving unsolicited advice, so let's just say that here are some lessons I've learned over the years about feeling beautiful.

How you dress is only half of it. Spend more time working on your character, being true to your values, such as integrity, kindness, and honesty, and becoming the person that you would be proud of than you spend on your wardrobe. Your character will define you and the outfits you wear will enhance the beautiful soul that you are.

Know that your values won't change much over time, but how you wish to express yourself will. Don't be afraid to experiment. Try on a few personality and clothing styles from time to time to see how they feel. Be true to yourself but be spirited and exotic as well. Have courage. Peer pressure (at any age) can be harsh, but your real tribe will always support you. And realize that feeling beautiful comes in waves – you might be hanging out in track pants, unmatched socks and unkempt hair, but the love of your friends at a fondue grill party will leave you feeling beautiful; conversely, you could be dressed to the nines, but a careless, hurtful word from your date could bring you down. Self-esteem and feeling beautiful are closely linked.

Finally, if you're having a bad hair day, and your skin is blotchy, and you've spilled your lunch into your lap, and you're just not feeling particularly pretty, just smile, pull your shoulders back, and remember your mantra: "I am still beautiful."

Kelly Wollf started C'est Sera Clothing Boutique in July 1, 2000 and the shoe department soon followed in 2002. In February 2017 C'est Sera added into Kelly Wollf into our selections. Her first Kelly Wollf store opened in August 2017 to carry the namesake of her own brand and create a mascot of sorts for people who love fashion and creatively put together the looks for their lives! Her team are experts in creating wardrobes and outfits that match who the customer is (or maybe wants to be!) The wolf of Kelly Wollf is mysterious, playful, sexy and strong. www.KellyWollf.com

****

I am Enough

By Ava Schriver Dunn

'Tub of Lard!' 'Hippo Hips!' 'Lard-Ass' 'Fatty'

And this wonderful tune that was so often sung to me in my childhood:

"Fatty, Fatty, two by four, couldn't get through the bathroom door, so she did it on the floor, licked it up and did some more!"

I've had these mean words thrown at me numerous times in my youth. I guess I can't adequately describe the level of pain caused by these seemingly innocuous, maybe even otherwise playful, innocent, words I shared above. It is indescribable, to a young-chubby-low-on-self-love-little-girl, the amount of hurt and insecurity that pervaded my little mind at the time, and hence, my not-so-little *Self*! The pain of which I would neither be able to fully comprehend, nor integrate, for what seemed like a lifetime.

People's outward expression of disgust towards the size and shape of my body didn't stop there. As a young 'chubby girl', trying to fit in and be accepted, while surrounded by a preponderance of skinny, petite, small-ass girls (literally) in my school, the plethora of tiny models on the covers of magazines that stared me in my chubby-cheeked-face on an almost daily basis (and now 24/7 with the advent of social media), was the most searing salt on a wound one could possibly imagine (or so it felt at the time!). I was inundated with the reminder that I wasn't 'pretty enough', 'skinny enough', 'lovable enough', '….enough' – each and every time I was standing in line at the grocery store I was being reminded, I suck! Thanks, media companies, for that not-so-gentle-reminder of my lack of self worth!

The long and short of it is, I was a 'fat', 'overweight', 'obese', 'chubby' little girl and thanks to the 80's *low fat, low calorie* diet phenomenon, and having overweight family members, I was introduced, from a much-too-young-age to the concept of 'losing weight'. I remember attending my first TOPS (Taking Off Pounds Sensibly) meeting at nine-years-old! No nine-year-old should ever be part of a TOPS meeting! God love those MUCH older, overweight gals who were there for emotional support from their peers as they took off pounds sensibly, but I was nine! And it wasn't just TOPS.

I was also introduced to Jane Fonda's workouts on VHS, which I tried quite unsuccessfully to achieve her tiny, Hollywood actress size body; and Weight Watchers, which I attended off and on. And there were others: dieticians, nutritionists, liquid diets (hey it worked for Oprah...*for a while*). The Cabbage Soup Diet. Starving myself. The Atkins Diet. I even gave Bulimia a serious attempt for years only to end up with destroyed teeth, an extra 100 pounds and one very hurt ego.

I was tormented by my overweight reality, deeply saddened by it, in fact, because I couldn't accept myself as a 'chubby little girl' and it didn't seem fair *I* had to be the one carrying around all this extra weight! Why couldn't I be the skinny one? The fit one? The pretty one? I was tormented by what felt like a never-ending battle with my body.

The inner turmoil unfolded, due to what felt like at the time, my unchangeable reality, was overwhelming to my fat-wish-I could-be-as-pretty-and-loveable-as-those-girls-on-TV-not-so-little Self. It upset me terribly back then; the reality I couldn't BE that beauty queen on television…I could only watch someone else win the prize.

The reality that I couldn't ever BE that figure skater because I wasn't born with the right sized body for it; the reality, I couldn't BE that dancer because my body wasn't designed for being flaunted on stage moving in such a physically outward, expressive way (the fat jiggled a little too much, you know?). The reality, I wasn't going to BE attractive to, and BE loved by a man one day because he wouldn't think I'm beautiful enough to BE loved. The supposed reality, I couldn't BE who I wanted to BE because it seemed I was surrounded by people and living in a world that told me I couldn't…that I wasn't enough…*but did they?*

I have been told by various people over the years – my sister who is 12 years my senior, my childhood school bus driver, friends of the family, to name a few - that I was a very happy child, always smiling, with a laugh that would make other people laugh out loud, and a certain kind-loving-Spirit that is unfortunately not common enough in the world nowadays, it seems. But how could this be true?

I didn't remember being a happy child growing up. I was miserable…*wasn't I?* I was depressed…*wasn't I?* I was lonely…*wasn't I?* You see, this idea I was a 'happy child' that these foolish people told me was the truth; did not align with my beliefs, so I couldn't understand how it could be true. This confused me because it was not how I remember my childhood.

I remember it being filled with pain, sorrow, and spending A LOT of time alone in that despondency…*right? Didn't I?* I know, I know. I was as confused as you are right now! But this was a fact I was now faced with, a part of the story I had either missed completely or totally forgot about! It had to be a grave mistake. It is not possible I was a happy child because I had so much to be UN-happy about!! How is it possible, people in my life at the time perceived me to be happy, when on the inside, I was filled with sadness?

It used to be, when I looked back on my life as a 'chubby child' I perceived it as this pained, hurt, sad, lonely experience I resented and always tried to wish away. My reality then, as I once perceived it, was filled with memories of a childhood-gone-wrong and one filled with pain from the harsh, outside world I was living in! How could the world be so cruel to a little girl who just wanted nothing more than to be loved? How could my family have not seen how much pain I was in?

Well, the answer was one I could not easily accept for some time, and in fact, it took me years to allow it to become a truth in my life, and that answer is simply this; because I wasn't in *that* much pain! I know, it was shocking to me too. I had spent a lifetime perceiving – believing - my childhood was riddled with pain and suffering. How could it be that all of a sudden I am acknowledging, outwardly admitting, *it wasn't that bad?* Well, because it wasn't! You see, we all perceive our lives through our filters, that play an integral role in how we perceive/make sense of OUR world. I had formed ideas in my mind based on past experiences and yes, I had some traumatic experiences growing up, but I had created these ideas in my mind that simply weren't true…or didn't have to be MY truth.

I, like so many had shaped my beliefs about myself based on what others told me about myself...*or what I perceived I was being told.* I believed things about myself that weren't true! They were just words–ideas–messages - told to me through the not so subtle images on magazine covers, in movies, through the written word and the verbally expressed meanness, from other children and various other (in)significant individuals in my life. Basically, the shit I was dealing with wasn't even mine, but I was taking it on as my own! I was causing my own inner conflict, creating more of my own internal pain, moreso by the *self*-judgment, than *any* condemnation I was getting from my outside world! The things I was saying to myself were far more damaging than anything I was being 'told' in my environment.

Woah! What's this?! Yes, that's right, I was taking personal responsibility for why I was feeling the way I was. I finally came to the realization that so long as I was willing to believe these limited ideas about myself and let others determine my self worth, I would never be happy. So I took control. I decided I am worth it to give myself that which I had been seeking 'out there' my entire life. I decided to stop blaming other – people, organizations, entities, the government, the weather, my father, whatever – for why I felt *less than* enough.

After a lot of self reflection, MANY pages of intensely, brutally, honest journal writing, consciously forgiving those whom I felt had done me wrong and most importantly, forgiving myself - it was in this deep gratitude for everyone playing the role they have in my life, regardless of the pain, that was instrumental in my letting the old perceived pain from my past go.

I learned the lessons from those 'bad' experiences and brought those new resources forward into a more awakened, healthy, happy and peaceful TRUE reality. I see my world from a whole new perspective now. Keep in mind, I acknowledge I did experience painful events in my life that certainly have contributed to the hurt I have felt over the years, BUT the revelation I have come to know is that I don't have to 'own' these beliefs.

I don't have to *believe* that I am not pretty, skinny, fit, beautiful enough. I can choose instead to not let what other people's opinions of me determine my self worth. I KNOW the only person who has to believe I am beautiful, is me. It's not up to my husband, my children, my family, friends, or the world, to tell me I'm beautiful. I just have to choose it.

The weight of the world was placed on me, by none other than me and nobody else, and it was never a physical weight after all…it was all in my mind. It was an emotional weight I took on and became my identity in this life. I never needed anyone else to tell me I am beautiful. As cliché as it sounds, I *was* the one I have been waiting for all along!

Now, it's important at this point to understand, I had not just one epiphany, but many epiphanies – or 'breakthroughs' - throughout my over 40 years, that have helped me to take the blinders off, remove the jaded glasses - filtered memories of my past and see, for the first time in my Life, the Truth. I was not what anyone had told me I was. I was, and AM, enough! And to top it off, I did, after all, find the courage to enter two beauty pageants in my late teens, both of which I won, still considered 'obese' at 200 pounds. Take that, Jane Fonda!

Ava Schriver Dunn is a trailblazer, idea catalyst, and people connector extraordinaire. As a gifted Intuitive Medium, Talk Show Host, Professional Speaker, and Natural Health Professional, Ava inspires, teaches, and motivates people into action - empowering them to experience Life to its fullest...and have fun doing it!

A conscious Entrepreneur and Humanitarian at heart, Ava is doing her part to end human suffering by helping individuals transform their health, become happier and more fulfilled human beings, adding to a more joyful, peaceful world for all of us. Ava lives by the mantra: If you want to change the world, you have to change yourself...first.
http://www.AvaSchriverDunn.com

****

How Could I....

By Kimberly Ann Rose

At forty-eight and a half years old I have been pondering writing my story to benefit someone out there on their own journey of this thing called 'life'. The question that always held me back was, "How could you of all people help anyone out there?" Then the FABULOUS Miss Kelly Falardeau whom I have known for over four years and has witnessed me overcome some life challenges asked me to share my life story in this book. So how could I not agree to this amazing opportunity, especially as a firm believer in that things happen for a reason. So here we go peeps.

How could I be a non-abusive parent to my own children if my father didn't beat me everyday worse than the last day?

How could I be encouraging not only to my own children, family, friends and clients if I was not emotionally, spiritually and mentally torn down to zero self-worth and self-confidence daily by my father?

How could I succeed in high school and college if I was not told endlessly how stupid and unproductive in life I would be? That I would probably never finish high school never mind think of attending college, daily from my father? Maybe this is where as an adult I can not seem to soak up enough knowledge. Remember my peeps, knowledge is something in you that no one can ever take from you!

How would I know what surviving was if my dad had not completely left my mom shut down and broken after she left him for good the fourteenth time? Mom would be confused mentally and emotionally; she would leave me alone at ten-years-old to fend for myself to return for a night or two with my dad or a late shift when she was capable to work. She would be so depressed and exhausted from life with him she would sleep for days on the couch. I watched her sleep and I would cry alone because I was so hungry and many times there was no food, heat or power. Yet I managed to get myself up, walk across the city to and from school only to come home and find her still sleeping.

How would I learn humility and what embarrassment was if my mother did not have the inability to be able to budget money while we were on welfare if I didn't have to apologize to business owners, my friend's parents and family members for her cheques bouncing faster than she could write them out or the fact she had stolen money from some of them? My father also helped with this lesson the day before grade one school pictures. With my thin, white, blonde hair so long, it was just passing the bottom of my bum he decided to gift me his famous hair cut my older brothers regularly received... a brush cut. I don't think I could explain the flash of different emotions that raced through my little body.

How would I learn the value of hard work when I got my first job at twelve to help out my mom because she was fired again from another job.

How would I learn what stress was in life as an adult and the effects of being poor if my mom still after months of me getting my first part-time job could not find work and I took it upon myself to get another part-time job? My days Monday to Friday were school for grade eight then straight to my dishwashing job and when that was done, walked over to my nightly babysitting job until after ten at night. Still not enough money for rent, bills, her smokes and food. It got so bad at home that at my second nightly job I started stealing food from them to take home to feed me and my mom. Still need to ask forgiveness for that one.

How could I know what determination and perseverance was if at the age of fifteen things were so bad at home with no money I would walk right into the local lawyer's office all alone and ask him to help me take my dad to court for child support? He agreed and a year later I was awarded child support. I remember my friends and even my mom's friends being so excited and proud for me. To me, I didn't see any of what they seen, it was just the only choice I had. Next time I take a trip home I should stop in and ask that lawyer what he thought of all that.

How could I comprehend PTSD, emotional and mental abuse or the long- term effects of this if I had not watched my mother take her last beating from my father that I was sure ended her life as she lay on the floor in a pool of her own blood with her false teeth broken in half on the floor beside her? Perhaps I also learned this lesson from the six men who sexually abused me from preschool to my teen years. Leaving me to believe that sex was only for the man's pleasure and it was not to be enjoyed or cherished in an adult relationship. That I was somehow a magnet for this evil and never to love or appreciate my body, sexuality or the touch of another and heaven forbid self-touch for the sake of one's own pleasure.

How could I not learn to trust my intuition if so many adult men and fake friends with their own personal agendas had not treated me with such disrespect and narcissism?

How would I learn forgiveness and compassion if four to five years ago I did not become aware my entire life had to happen just the way it did to accept these were actually gifts of lessons that turned into blessings beyond what I could imagine or comprehend of what was yet to come for me? I even had to forgive my grandmother that said she should have not been so righteous to send my mom back to my dad every time she came looking for help from her.

How could I now use all these horrible lessons to assist and create my calling and purpose of gifts given to me as an intuitive energetic healer and now of recent, an empowerment leadership coach for organization, teams, professionals, families and one on one if I did not experience them all first hand and know truly what each of these lessons felt like spiritually, emotionally, physically and mentally?

How could I do this without three key things most of us never believe we have, could use, or that these are things we should listen to, follow and ask countless questions to ourselves which is our very own INTUITION, AWARENESS and CHOICE?

How could I express to you how amazing my life is with these gifts, abilities and tools bestowed to me to assist others on their very own journey of life.

I could have easily told myself I'm going to use the victim card and given up. From that first painful childhood memory to recently ending my second marriage and becoming a single parent. Are you kidding me...I cannot wait to come into contact with those struggling in all the areas I survived and more, to gift them a life line from daily funk and junk to PTSD of combat and non-combat. Yes... me I am helping people all over the world!

How can I be this blessed after all of this to love my life every day more than the day before? It is beyond amazing, let me tell you. How does it get any better than this? How did I get so lucky to be me? What would it take for me to create even more amazingness around the world to other souls? What else is possible that I have not even considered or have comprehension that I can create? These are questions I ask myself every day that YOU can ask yourself many times in a day peeps.

How could you not believe you have a purpose in life after hearing my story? Struggling to find that purpose? Contact me and I will assist you.

Don't get me wrong, not everyday is awesome for me. It is my very own choice to create an awesome day. Sometimes it takes sitting in the awareness of yuck and pain longer than other days as I need to get the lesson from it. That is okay, honour your awareness for what you are feeling, then use your intuition, create your choice to change. Not your spouse's choice or your parents, co-workers or friends… that is the power of YOU not to be given to anyone else ever. Asking questions to other people and assessing that information is great; then pick apart all the stuff that feels right and light to you and your intuition. An amazing tool I use in my healings and coaching sessions is if it feels light in your tummy, it is right for you. If it feels heavy in your tummy, it is not right for you. Just to clarify, because this is very important, so listen up peeps. If you ask someone a question and their light and heavy is not the same as yours, that does not make you right and them wrong or vice versa. What that means is, their truth for their being is just different than yours, nothing more or less. This awareness allows you the amazingness of 'non-judgement' which is so peaceful to have in life. Non-judgement gifts give us such ease and peace within our own life. I could not use the gifts, tools and abilities I have been gifted or studied to assist others if I had judgement.

Wishing you all a life of ease, non-judgement, joy, awareness, intuition and choice. Remember Bgood2U always me peeps.

Kimberley Ann Rose *is known to her family, friends, colleagues and clients as just Kimmy. She gifts the world her energy of unique charm, humor, sassiness with a slight sprinkle or more of princess (either self-sprinkled or sprinkled from the universe) along with her genuine elegance of kindness and compassion for those she meets. So, it is fitting that when she opened her business as an Energetic Intuitive Healer and Empowerment Coaching she called it, none other than 'KimmyEnergy'. Kimmy's three favorite sayings are, 'challenge accepted', 'just me being me' and 'you can't make this shit up my peeps'. She is a champion of heartache, survival, determination, horrific childhood traumas*

(physically, mentally, emotionally, spiritually and sexually), perseverance and PTSD. Her gift is to teach and assist souls how to become aware of their very own awareness, intuition and choice. Encouraging souls to become more than they ever thought possible then living as a victim. You can follow her at KimmyEnergy.com or on Facebook & Instagram by liking her pages KimmyEnergy Potency of Choice.
www.KimmyEnergy.com

Feeling powerless over food?

It's time to get free & vibrant!

Join us on a 90-day Health Challenge that will fuel your body & soul and nourish your spirit & mind.

Mention the Still Beautiful Book & Receive 30% off - 90-day Health & Wellness Challenge

www.WildNewLife.com
email: admin@VibrantNewLife.com

Vibrant New Life.
Holistic Coaching & Consulting
Life is what you make it, so let's make it good!

"let food be thy medicine and medicine be thy food." Hippocrate

By learning how to be a great speaker, presenter, and storyteller, you will literally open doors to amazing opportunities for yourself...and I want to show you how.

5 Steps to Becoming a Successful Speaker

To register for Eric Edmeades' 5-day Mini Speaking Course, go to: https://bit.ly/2ELplLS

Every woman deserves to have a beautiful portrait
for personal branding, for a family legacy
or simply because you are worthy.

www.ALLISONORTHNER.com

WOULD YOU LIKE TO HOST A...

Still Beautiful
MOVIE NIGHT?

And/Or book Kelly to speak at your event.

Go to:
www.KellyFalardeau.com or
www.StillBeautifulDoc.com

Still *Beautiful*
The Kelly Falardeau Story
(Speaker | Author | Coach)

Check out Kelly's
latest products:

https://www.zazzle.ca
/kelly_falardeau

To sponsor or purchase your own blanket, go to
www.BlanketsForBurnKids.com

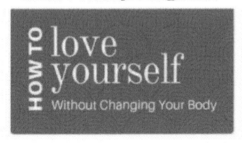

To access the FREE Case Study: How I Wrote & Published a Book in 3 Easy Steps in 3 Days & How You Can Too....

Click: http://bit.ly/CaseStudyPublishBook

About Kelly Falardeau

Kelly Falardeau is a 4x Best-Selling Author, Documentary Producer, Artist, Award-Winning Motivational Speaker and single mother. Friends, family and those who have worked with Kelly all say that she doesn't let fear stop her – when she wants to achieve something, she just does it. They also say the fact that Kelly is a burn survivor since she was two-years-old is so motivating because she does not let circumstances dictate her success.

At 21, she was nominated and won the position of President of the Alberta Burn Rehabilitation Society. As a kid, she also won the 4-H Most Improved Member award plus various public speaking awards and even the fastest senior typist award in high school.

Kelly has been featured on TV around the world, such as Global TV Edmonton and Calgary, CTS TV, CTV TV, Breakfast TV, Access TV, CBC, A-Channel and CFRN. She has also appeared as a guest on various radio shows too. Articles have been written about her in the Edmonton Woman Magazine, Edmonton Examiner, Edmonton Journal, Edmonton Sun, Pioneer Balloons Balloon Magazine and she also won the MOM Executive Officer award plus the Fierce Woman of the Year award from the MOM Magazine, YWCA Woman of Distinction 2013 and Queen Elizabeth II Diamond Jubilee medal.

Kelly was chosen amongst thousands to present her business to the Dragons for the Dragons' Den television. Kelly was selected out of 1500-women to compete in the Every Woman model search competition. She faced her fear of being judged by her appearance and walked the plank and won the Peoples' Choice award.

She is a sought–after international TEDx speaker because of her ability to engage others. She is able to move audience's emotions and make them see how a bad situation can become a great one. She will have you crying, laughing and dancing in your chairs as she shares her many stories about risks/rewards, inner beauty and self-esteem. Her beauty exercise is a dynamite experience that shows teenagers and adults where their true beauty comes from. She is also the author of 'No Risk No Rewards', 'Self Esteem Doesn't Come in a Bottle' (made the bestseller list in one day), 1000 Tips for Teenagers, 7 Ways to Embrace the Real You and now Still Beautiful which was produced into a documentary about her life story.

To book Kelly for your next event, email her at admin@KellyFalardeau.com or visit her website at: www.KellyFalardeau.com

Made in the USA
Lexington, KY
05 November 2019